Two Readers
A Colorful Enantiodromia
Reading the Mysteries of Your Other Self

Two Readers

A Colorful Enantiodromia

Reading the Mysteries of Your Other Self

by

Peter Daino

BP

TWO READERS:
A Colorful Enantiodromia
Reading the Mysteries of Your Other Self

by
Peter Daino

© Copyright 2003 by Peter Daino
First Edition, 2003.

Library of Congress Control Number: 2003105433
ISBN#: 1-892451-04-2

Published by
Brundage Publishing
74 Front Street
Binghamton, N.Y. 13905

Illustration Credits:
"R.G. Marie" by Debbie Morello, "Chat Corner" by Brian Zampier,
and "Ibis" artwork by Michael Bugara

Cover/Book Design:
Ahead Publishing House
Endicott, NY 13760

Printed in the United States of America.

This book is dedicated to the Society of Mary,
to the Family Rosary Apostolate of the Holy Cross,
to the Brothers of St. Charles Lwanga,
and
to all who teach literacy to poor children in Africa.

They learned pedagogy for the oppressed from the martyred
"Proto-Reader of East Africa," Charles Lwanga,*
whose reading of the Gospel emboldened him to stand up to a
tyrant, whose reading is freedom.

---

* St. Charles Lwanga, Leader of the Ugandan Martyrs (1885), was killed by the King of Uganda for reading and teaching others to read the Gospel.

Acknowledgments

I want to acknowledge the people and places that made this book possible. First, I thank Nairobians and Nairobi. Reading you for seventeen years has been the most inspiring and formative experience I've ever had. I've never encountered anywhere else in the world as much imagination and creativity.

Second, I thank the Society of Mary in the United States of America and in Africa. Your encouragement made all the difference. The Marian Community we share is the vessel, the treasure chest that contains the meanings I cherish for my life.

Third, I thank my family. My mother and father gave me the gift of faith, and the second most valuable thing in my life: the ability to read.

Fourth, I thank the Family Rosary, especially Fr. Phalen and Laeititia.

I'll stop numbering now and just list the numerous people and places I want to thank:

Franklin Resseguie and Rebecca Loomis at Brundage Publishing without whose professional assistance this book could not have been published; M. H. (Behrooz) Tamdgidi at Ahead Publishing House who designed the book cover and text; Debbie Morello, the main illustrator of this Book along with Brian Zampier and Michael Bugara who each did an illustration; The Camoldolese Nuns at Transfiguration Monastery in Windsor, New York; Original Readers of the manuscript: Paul Landolfi, SM, Johann Roten, SM, Steve Glodek, SM, Katherine Ashe, John Phalen, CSC; The Marianist Community in Malawi; My next-door neighbors in Endwell, N.Y. – Mike and Chris Zick who let me use their word processor and were always so gracious; All the enchanted places in Africa where I sat, and read, and daydreamed; All the less enchanted places, even sitting on long bus rides in Kenya and Malawi (one time to make a photocopy of this manuscript I took a bus ride that totaled eighteen hours); All the students at Chaminade Secondary School in Karonga, Malawi;

God for giving me energy to write four hours a day (before morning prayer) six days a week from 1992-1999 and for giving me forms and themes; God for the M.I.R.A.C.L.E. my mother said would come when hers did not.

Peter Daino, S.M.,
Karonga, Malawi, Africa, April 2003

Two Readers

Introducing the Text

Liberita

My name is Liberita. I am your host through the pages of this book. Let me tell you about myself and about the book.

I grew up in one of Nairobi's slums. I'm the eldest of three orphans. We were all illiterate. I learned to read and write first. Then I taught my siblings.

Agio taught me to read and write.

Rama tried to save the life of my little brother.

But wait, I am getting ahead of the story.

What you need to know now is that having learned to read and write I interviewed for a job at the Wasomaji newspaper. And I was hired.

That was in 1999. And do you know who hired me?

The founder and first editor of the Wasomaji hired me. Her name is Naibis. Now let me tell you about her, the newspaper, and how this book came to be.

Naibis is a book supplier in Nairobi. She sells and delivers books to the major bookstores in the city. Readers' Guide (owned by Lwanga, a very dear friend of hers) was one of the bookstores she supplied.

Editing is something Naibis does on the side. She is not paid for putting out the Wasomaji. It does not require that much work really. It's just an eight page weekly.

Wasomaji means Readers. It is a community owned newspaper. The Circle of Readers owns it. And they submit articles to it. The articles have to be on the practice of Lectio.

Lectio is divine reading, a form of meditation in which Nairobi is integrated with the reading of beads: green ones for joy and red ones for sorrow.

Naibis founded the Wasomaji in 1963; the year Kenya gained its independence. She was editor of the paper until the end of the century.

During most of the years Naibis edited the paper there was a split in the Circle of Readers. The split involved two factions:

those who read only sorrow (red) in the world (angry fighters), and those who read only joy (green) in the world (serene contemplatives). Their dispute appeared in the Wasomaji as features, essays, and poems. The fiercest years of dispute were from 1979 to 1994.

When Naibis was about to retire she asked me to be her successor. I told her I would do it under one condition. I said that I would be the new editor of Wasomaji only after the publication of the book you are holding.

She agreed. In fact, she seemed more enthusiastic about the undertaking than I was.

We pored over old issues of the Wasomaji and selected the texts, which make up this book. We questioned each text: Does it show the nature of the controversy? Does it tell the story of the conflict? Does it have a good reason for being in this anthology? Many texts were discarded after such questioning. What you have in hand are the most essential texts.

We also went through our files of unpublished articles. Naibis stopped them from being published at the time they were written in order to protect certain people. But now it hurts no one, and indeed, helps many for these articles to appear now in the story of Two Readers.

As I said above, I am your host through the pages of the book. At the beginning of each of the four parts and in a few other places I'll have something to tell you. Naibis also makes a few editorial comments. (What else do you expect in a collection of newspaper articles assembled by the editors of that very newspaper? The temptation was too hard for us to resist.)

Naibis and I hope that wherever our comments appear in this book we've helped the Two Readers – Agio and Rama – relay in an integrated way the story that many of you (in the Circle of Readers) have been longing to read from beginning to end.

May the anthology you hold in your hand – whether you be a Redbead or a Greenbead – open your mind to that textual joy or that textual passion which you steadfastly avoided in the first half of your reading life.

May the Power of Enantiodromia be with you.

Introducing Mary

Liberita

When we collected the texts that make up this anthology, Naibis and I were thinking of the Circle of Nairobi Readers. We had in mind those who practice lectio with rosary in hand; and they, of course, already understand why we call Mary the Readers' Guide.

But, having finished our manuscript, we've now decided to say something here about Mary as Readers' Guide for the sake of the person who does not belong to the Circle of Nairobi Readers and may never have heard Mary called the Readers' Guide, and yet, somehow, (by the grace of God?) find themselves holding this anthology with wonder and curiosity.

Why is Mary called "Readers' Guide?"

There are five reasons:

1. Through her reading it the Word became flesh: Mary's flesh, Human flesh.

2. Mary taught the Word (the boy Jesus) to read.

3. Mary compiled the traditional 15 mysteries of the rosary. The rosary, you could say, is a kind of anthology of all the gospels. (Now that Naibis and I have become anthologists ourselves we appreciate the hard work Mary did when she strung together 15 holy stories to make a rosary).

4. Mary symbolizes Wisdom. In the Catholic reading of the Old Testament Mary is Sophia who was present with the Creator when each and every thing was given its character. She also knows how each and everything yearns for wholeness; longs to become its opposite.

5. Mary helps us to read the future.

We needn't say more about the first reason. All Christians believe that the Word was made incarnate through Mary's "Yes." Mary practiced lectio, so intensely that the Word she read became her very flesh and blood.

That Mary taught the Word to read, to speak, to see, to touch, to feel, to hear, to smell, to know the world – this is the source of great wonder. Before the incarnation God never read with human eyes, never spoke with a human voice, never touched with human fingers, never could feel, hear, smell, or know the world in a human way. Mary gave God the capacity to read the creation with human senses. The Readers' Guide taught the Creator to read the Creation. What a privilege to have such a teacher. The very one who made God sensuous now makes us so, teaches us, as she taught Christ, to read with all our senses this creation, teaches us *literasee*.

Mary compiled the fifteen mysteries of the rosary. We all weave the events of our lives together into a narrative. For some people the narrative is full of sorrow. For others the narrative is full of joy. What makes Mary's compilation special is that she integrated all the diverse stories of her life together in such a way that anyone who reads the whole rosary learns to participate with joy in the sorrows of the world. And that, according to the great mythologist Joseph Campbell, is the glorious life of bliss.

Allow us another paragraph on the rosary. It is essential to this book that you understand the rosary as fifteen hero stories. The first five hero stories are about the childhood of Jesus. Mary probably told these stories to the adolescent Jesus so that he would see himself as a hero. (Mothers love to tell stories, which show teen-agers that they were hero-children. This helps the teens to believe in themselves.) Mary told the next five hero stories to the apostles to show them that they could handle their crosses as Jesus did his. Mary told the last five hero stories to St. Dominic (when she gave him the whole anthology). The people of Dominic's time, when a third of Europe's population died of the Bubonic Plague, needed those final mysteries of the rosary to imagine the dead, the millions and millions of dead, in glory. The fifteen stories, which Mary strung together, are mediums of power. The rosary is a chaplet for champions; it will help you to see and love your hero-self.

Mary is Sophia. She is the Lady of Enantiodromia. What is that you ask? Enantiodromia is the yearning for wholeness, the desire in a thing to become its opposite. Both the Joyful Reader and the Sorrowful Reader are everywhere yearning for wholeness; each desires the opposite. And through the Lady of Enantiodromia one can indeed *read the mysteries of one's other self.*

Mary helps us read the future. How? Simply by looking at her. She is the Second Eve. What the First Eve started – the human project – Mary completes. That is why the Church celebrates Mary as Assumpta. In this figure (described in the book of Revelation as the Queen crowned with twelve stars) we see the end point of our evolution; we see that the lowly one Mary spoke of in her Magnificat is raised up; the last is made first. Maria Assumpta is the Icon of the Church Triumphant.

I have tried to explain why we call Mary the Readers' Guide. It will become clearer as you continue to read. And so, from now on, we shall refer to her as R. G. Marie. You know now that "R" is for Reader and "G" is for Guide.

May she guide you in reading this book.

May she who gave the Word body, making it readable, make this body, this book, and everybody readable.

R. G. Marie

She ate and drank the precious words,

her spirit grew robust;

She knew no more that she was poor,

Nor that her frame was dust.

She danced along the dingy days,

And this bequest of wings

Was but a book. What liberty

A loosened spirit brings.

—Emily Dickinson

The Traditional* Mysteries of the Rosary

The Green Mysteries:

The Annunciation
The Visitation
The Nativity of the Lord
The Presentation of Jesus in the Temple
The Finding of the Lost Child

The Red Mysteries:

The Agony in the Garden
The Scourging at the Pillar
The Crowning with Thorns
The Carrying of the Cross
The Crucifixion and Death of Our Lord

The Glorious Mysteries:

The Resurrection
The Ascension of Christ into Heaven
The Descent of the Holy Spirit upon the Apostles
The Assumption of the Blessed Virgin into Heaven
The Coronation of the Blessed Virgin Mary in Heaven

> *God has counted in fifteen Mysteries,*
> *on the fingers of human creatures,*
> *the singleness of the undivided Love,*
> *the simplicity*
> *that we cannot comprehend*
> *because our hearts are divided.*
> *Caryll Houselander*

---

* In the rosary's thousand year history there has always been freedom to choose another mystery of Christian faith and put it under Green, Red, or Glorious. In this book, Readers add and subtract mysteries, exercising this freedom.

Cast of Characters

Agio -   An artist who enjoys loafing. He is the leader of the Greenbeads.

Liberita - Yours truly. An illiterate girl from the slums who becomes the editor of a newspaper and of this book.

Lwanga -   Owner and manager of a bookstore in Nairobi, Kenya. His bookstore is named Reader's Guide. His supplier is Naibis. He keeps the Ibis.

Naibis -   An old woman; a writer; a book supplier; an "odd bird;" the founder and first editor of the *Wasomaji*. Her name is derived from blending the words Nairobi and ibis.

Rama -   A medical doctor whose expertise is immunology. He is the manager of a blood bank for children. He is the leader of the Redbeads.

Part One

The Conflict Begins

Why I Walked Out and Took the Redbeads with Me

Rama, Wasomaji, May 1979[1]

In the past few weeks there has been much speculation about a group of Readers who walked out of the most recent reading of the joyful mysteries at Lwanga's store. As the leader of the walkout that Saturday morning I want to give the reason why we left. The best way to do this is to describe the scene.

As usual the bead reading began at ten in the morning. A candle was lit near the statue of R. G. Marie. There were about sixty readers assembled. We began by singing "With What Joy We Sing of Mary." Fine. Agio was the leader of the reading that Saturday and he introduced the first joyful mystery, the Annunciation.

"Let us picture R. G. Marie," said the artist, "As she waits for the archangel. There she is, sitting, at leisure. There she is, attentive and watching, ready to receive. And here we are, fellow Readers, at leisure, and ready to receive. Hail Mary, full of grace. The Lord is with you. Blessed are you..."

Typical Agio stuff; leisure, receptivity, sponginess. Don't get me wrong – there is nothing harmful about picturing R. G. Marie

---

[1] *Rama, Wasomaji, May 1979*: this means that "Why I Walked Out and Took the Redbeads with Me" first appeared as an article in the weekly eight-page newspaper Wasomaji (Readers) in May 1979 and was written by Rama.

as passive, sitting, ready to receive, though many of us would prefer different adjectives for this zealous young woman. I sometimes wonder if she wrestled with the angel at the Annunciation. Jacob did, and it left a mark on him. We know that she debated with the angel, "How can this be?" In any case, when the Readers finished the first decade, Agio introduced the second.

"Picture R. G. Marie at noon when the sun is bright and warm. Forget the dark, cold cave and the night. She gives birth in a cheerful room with sunlight streaming through open windows. The shepherds play their pipes and Joseph dances around the room with the newborn child in his arms. Hail Mary, full of grace..."

I couldn't say the second half of the prayer. I tried it, "Holy Mary, Mother of God pray for us sinners..." but the words got stuck. With Agio's image of noonday piping and dancing in mind I couldn't say "...and at the hour of our death." I looked around at others in the bookstore and noticed I was not alone. Many other Readers were unable to pray.

"The Third Joyful Mystery, the Visitation," intoned Agio. It irritated me that he was arranging the mysteries to suit himself. Why must he make the second into the third? What was his point?

The sycophant went on, "Much too much is made of the Magnificat by Liberation Theology. Of course R. G. Marie said that the mighty would be brought down from their thrones. The point, though, is that the lowly would be seated on thrones. In splendor we will sit, like R. G. Marie, magnifying Eternal light. This, by God's doing, not ours. Readers are to give in, enjoy, taste the sweetness of..."

I stopped listening and shook my head. I saw others were also shaking their heads. Agio had desecrated a sacred piece of scripture. At the Visitation R. G. Marie is the Prophet of Liberation.

She sees the tables turned on the mighty *bwanas*[2]. R. G. Marie sees a world of justice where the hungry take good things and eat.

---

[2] *Bwana* – Lord, Boss.

Agio is wrong! The Magnificat is not sitting, inaction, and surrender.

By the time the third decade was finished I had already put my beads in my pocket. I couldn't pray with Agio, but I didn't intend a disturbance. But he made it impossible for me... "The Fourth Joyful Mystery, The Holy Family Dance Disco at the *Nyama Choma*[3]. Don't be surprised, fellow Readers. The Temple in those ancient days was the place of festivity. There was music and dancing and plenty of meat. Picture Jesus Mary and Joseph at leisure in the *Nyama Choma*, celebrating..."

That is when I walked out. I had been force fed enough green to last me a lifetime.

Marching out of the bookstore I observed the reaction of other Readers. And if I noticed anyone standing and looking toward the door, I pulled him or her by the hand. "Let's get out of here," I shouted. And thus thirty of us walked out together.

That was the day when we, who now call ourselves Redbeads, resolved never to return to a joyful reading of the rosary.

Why I Walked Out and Took the Greenbeads with Me

Agio, Wasomaji, June 1979

Though the group now calling itself Redbeads stormed out of a reading of the joyful mysteries last month, we, whom they insulted, still attended the reading of the sorrowful mysteries this month. Faithful to our obligations! Good Readers attend all the bead readings – whether of the joy, the sorrow, or the glory.

Yes, we attended only to be insulted again. That is why we had to walk out. Let me describe the scene to you, dear Readers, so that you can judge rightly about these Redbeads who have destroyed the confraternity of the rosary in Nairobi.

The bead reading began at 10 AM this past Saturday. A candle

---

[3] *Nyama Choma* – A Kenyan-style beer hall where goat meat is eaten.

was lit near the statue of R. G. Marie. About sixty Readers were assembled. The opening song was the Stabat Mater, an appropriate choice for the reading of the sorrowful mysteries. Rama, the prayer leader, introduced the first sorrow.

"Massacre of the Innocents! The sorrows begin here. Do you know that today 40,000 children will die on planet earth from hunger or a disease that should have been prevented by vaccine? Here in Nairobi, the infant mortality rate is almost one hundred per thousand births. Here in the capital of the most advanced country in East Africa! Herod acted out of jealousy. And us? We don't act because of our indifference. Hail Mary, full of grace. The Lord is with you. Blessed are you among women and blessed is the fruit of your womb, Jesus – the sole innocent to survive and who now vindicates his age mates."

Grand theatrics! And for what? To make Readers feel guilty. The sorrow beads are not to be used as a whip. That is what I was thinking as I prayed the first ten.

"The second mystery: Refugee Children. During this decade let us meditate on the child Jesus as a refugee in Africa. He did spend some years here with that label. What are we doing for our child refugees, be they our own displaced nationals, or foreigners who flee to Kenya from Somalia, Sudan, or Ethiopia? Hail Mary..."

Is this prayer? It sounds more like a newscast. We know there are problems in the world. But how long can we endure a journalist who manipulates our religious emotions? Who does he think he is? And where did he get permission to invent new sorrow mysteries? It is okay to change the order of the mysteries but this Rama is adding... "Third mystery..."

He is already onto the third! I was distracted through the entire second mystery. I'm not able to pray with Rama.

"Third mystery; The Pieta. Look there at the deathbed of the child with measles, or whooping cough, or tuberculosis, or diphtheria. Look there at R. G. Marie holding the child in her arms.

"What is she thinking? That these are preventable diseases!

That something could have been done? This year, 1979, the United Nations is designating 'Year of the Child.' Let us promise to do this year what must be done. Hail Mary..."

I look around in the bookstore at other Readers. Some are shaking their heads. Maybe they are wondering, as I am, if this is prayer or propaganda. I didn't come to Reader's Guide to hear a UNICEF bulletin read to me. I just cannot get into this. I put my beads away. I really don't want to walk out, though. It will appear vindictive. People will think I'm doing it because of what happened last month. But I can't take much more of Rama's preaching.

"The fourth sorrowful mystery: R. G. Marie standing at the foot of the cross. Did you hear what I said Readers? She is standing at the foot of the cross. She is not sitting, she is not running away. She is standing tall and brave. R. G. Marie is not afraid of suffering. She stands beside the one who suffers. Do you see? She stands beside the child with polio being carried in a wheelbarrow through the muddy byways of Korogocho; she stands beside the child in the overcrowded standard three class who hasn't seen a book since entering primary school; she stands beside the child picking through the garbage dumpster. The garbage dumpster - a good allegory for Nairobi. This world is not a pretty place you see..."

I got to my feet. I looked around and saw others on their feet. I nodded to them. And we all headed toward the exit. There were about thirty of us. We didn't share Rama's disdain for creation, his garbagistic worldview. We resolve never to return to a sorrowful reading of the beads.

Agio, the Young Artist

Editors' note:

"Agio: Ancestors and Early Years" was written by Naibis during the period of "Cold War" between Greens and Reds that ensued after the 1979 breakup of the Circle of Readers. It has remained unpublished until now.

"Joyful Mysteries, According to a Young Artist" is a series of articles written by Agio himself during 1979 following the breakup of the Circle of Readers. This vocation story was published in the Wasomaji in late 1979 and widely circulated among the Greenbeads.

AGIO: ANCESTORS AND EARLY YEARS

Naibis, 1979

Agio is a Nairobian. He was born at the King George Hospital in Westlands on the 7th of October 1947. His mother was Kikuyu and his father was Italian.

His parents met during the Second World War. Agio's father, a captain who was fifty-two years old and near retirement, was taken prisoner, along with his command of Italian infantry, when the British army invaded southern Ethiopia in August 1943. He and his men occupied the POW camp just north of Nairobi. For their work duty they were made to construct the Naivasha Road.

In early 1944, Agio's father fell from a cliff at the Limuru escarpment. His road crew had been clearing brush there to make it possible for the steam shovel to drive up to that high point of the plateau situated at the precipice of the Rift Valley. The fall nearly killed him but he survived after forfeiting an irreparable leg to the surgeon's knife.

Agio's mother was a teacher, also older, not quite forty, and unmarried. She was hired by the colonial government in late 1944 to give the prisoners one lesson a week in English. She was, at the time, a full time teacher of literature at the Holy Ghost Fathers high school in St. Austin's Parish, Westlands.

Agio's father, a widower, fell in love with English. He would stay after class and discuss grammar with his teacher. After half a year he began to show her little English poems he had written. The first poems were about the highland trees and flowers of Limuru. Then came the love poems. Toward the end of the war the old captain asked his English teacher to marry him.

She didn't give him an answer for two weeks because her family was opposed to the idea. They found three weaknesses in the man she loved. Being Italian, he was of a different race. Being lame, he would not be much of a breadwinner. Being old, he would not even last a score of years. The first and second weaknesses, as far as Agio is concerned, turned out to be strengths. The third, alas, turned out to be true.

Against the wishes of her family the English teacher married her poem-writing student a week after the war ended. They were married in a quiet ceremony at St. Austin's Church. Their married life was like a fairy tale. Happiness was a constant flame that warmed their home. Sounds of laugher and music were never wanting in Kileleshwa, where they lived with their only child until 1964 when Agio's father died peacefully in his sleep at the age of seventy-three. Young Agio was still mourning the loss of his father when his mother, also passed away so overcome was she by grief. They buried her at St. Austin's cemetery beside her husband, whose grave was hardly a month old.

That same year Agio completed Form Six and he could have gone on to the University. The accident compensation money the government paid into his father's estate would continue for another five years. It would have been sufficient for fees. But Agio decided not to go on. (Later he would attend an art course for a few months but it became too demanding and he dropped out).

Soft is a word some would have used to describe the corpulent sixteen-year-old. Like his father he loved trees and flowers and spent much of his time on long walks in the countryside. He would play his flute in the fields or sit under a tree and read the poets his mother had taught at the Holy Ghost School. He especially liked Keats. His favorite poem was *Endymion*.

Joyful is another word that described Agio well. He had inherited a spirit of fun and a sense of humor from his parents. Though he grieved much when they died, he eventually recovered the *joie de vivre* that he cherished as an inheritance.

Agio was a sensitive young man but not a moper. He had a zest for the everyday but was not ambitious enough to plan tomorrow. So at sixteen he decided he was ready for life. He didn't need a University degree.

In fact, Agio was ready for the kind of life he wanted. He was not a possessive type of person and could live comfortably on a moderate income. The only thing he really asked of life was playtime – the days, the weeks, the months, however many were allotted him to contemplate the excessive beauty all around him.

Agio was religious in a non-conventional way. Although he attended mass every Sunday at St. Austin's, he was otherwise not involved in parish life. He didn't get much out of sermons and popular piety. He had his own way with the treasury of mystical experiences that had taken young Agio to Joys he thought beyond the reach of human beings.

Agio had no friends. He was happier in his own company, and preferred to be left alone. He didn't despise people – he liked them quite a lot. He was always thinking about them. He just didn't want to talk to them.

Agio might never have opened up – to people, to life, to the world – if it had not been for Lwanga. Yes, Agio "the artist" might never have hatched if it had not been for the Ibis-Keeper.

I am Agio, Leader of the Greenbeads

Agio, Wasomaji, December 8, 1979

I am a man of leisure. Of true leisure. I paint for a few hours in the morning, then I walk for an hour in the park. For lunch I eat fried plantain with a tasty sauce. Then I nap for two hours. By then it is time for afternoon tea. I like to take it on the porch and read Shelley. In the evenings I go to plays or concerts. This is my life. It is cultivated and tended like a garden.

I am not poor like many artists. I have a comfortable income. My paintings sell well and I am able to buy the books I want. I spend some money for rent and food, too, but not much. At the end of the month I always have a surplus. I bank it for a rainy day, though to tell you the truth I hardly think of tomorrow.

My friends in the Circle of Readers describe me in many ways:

Guru of Art for Art's Sake
Bohemian
Loafer
Mchezaji, or Lover of Play

Some call me the Oscar Wilde of Nairobi. I don't object to that name either. Speaking of that happy humorist of the 19th century I should admit that I look a bit like him. I am tall and round and heavy. And, as Wilde, I surprise people because even though I'm heavy I have an air about me that is light. People call me (as they did Wilde) the "Child."

I am very devoted to the Joyful Mysteries of the Rosary. They are all about the child Jesus. These mysteries show us the child in his leisure years at Nazareth. There, R. G. Marie taught him to read a world of simple joys.

Agio is my name. You should say it softly, pronounce it, A-dji-o. In Italian it means Leisure. I am the leader of those whose lives are cultivated gardens, those who love Nazareth. I am the leader of the Greenbeads.

Many of you have asked me, "How did you discover your vocation to be an artist?" Others have asked me, "How did you discover your vocation to be our leader?"

Over the next few weeks, you will be able to read in serial form the answers to these two questions. In the Christmas season of 1979/1980, the Year of the Child, the *Wasomaji* is dedicating several issues to the story of my vocational calling, and a series of articles entitled: "Joyful Mysteries According to a Young Artist" which details my calling as the leader of the Greenbeads.

Greenbeads, at Christmas, you and I kneel with the Three Magi before the Child in the manger, and we offer there the treasure of astronomers: sparkling eyes full of wonder and awe.

Come, Greenbeads, to Bethlehem, and kneel with me by the crib in the stardust. Behold the Creator is a creature now for your delight, so that you can play with him in your arms.

Be like R. G. Marie who never turned her gaze from *Bambino Divino*: The Good, The True, and The Beautiful in human form.

Greenbead Initiation (I)

Agio, Wasomaji, December 15, 1979

Lwanga was a friend of my father. It was because of my father that I met the Reader's Guide. Let me tell you what happened in those October days of 1963.

For weeks I had been complaining to my father about Nairobi. "I want to go to Italy," I said. "There are more beautiful things there than here. I wish I had not been born in Africa. Nothing here attracts me."

My father said, "You are purposely looking not to see."

"What?"

"Son, I am not the person who can help you see Nairobi. You won't let me. But I want you to meet someone who can help you *purposely look to see* the beauty here. Kenya has as much of it to see as Italy, even more."

When we reached the bookstore my father pointed up at the rainbow sign. Above the door I read the letters "R-E-A-D-E-R-S' G-U-I-D-E."

My father opened the store door and I walked inside.

"Who do we have here?" said Lwanga as he came up to me and shook my hand.

"This is my son, Agio," said my father closing the door behind him. He limped up to us and put his hands on top of our handshake.

"Son, I would like you to meet Mr. Lwanga. Do you know which saint he is named after?"

"Yes, Father," I said. "St. Charles Lwanga is one of the Ugandan Martyrs."

The Reader's Guide put his hand on my shoulder. "Do you know what else St. Charles Lwanga is famous for?"

"No," I said.

"He was the first youth in East Africa to read God's Word."

"Really?" I said.

"Well," said Lwanga, laughing. "That is always what I say when I introduce myself to young readers like you."

"I am happy my father introduced us," I said.

"So am I," said Lwanga. "Is there anything special I can do for you today?"

"Yes, as a matter of fact, there is," I said. "I am planning to leave Kenya. I want to go to Italy, my father's native land. I want to go there because I am seeking beauty. My father says that Kenya is just as beautiful, but I am looking purposely not to see. Maybe my father is right, but probably he is wrong. What have you to say?"

"Every place is readable. Places here, places there. The place is not the issue. No matter where you are, you will need to know how to read. How you read, that is the issue."

"But I do know how… Of course, I know how to read."

"If you really knew how to read," said Lwanga, "you would not feel this frantic need to leave the place in which you are to read beauty."

Lwanga took his hand off my shoulder. "Please, Agio, let me continue what I was saying." He put both hands behind his back and swayed up and down on the green carpet where he was standing. He was looking up at the ceiling, and talking in a low voice almost as if he was musing to himself. "Every place is readable. I always carry a book, my journal, and a pen. I always manage to find a spot for reading and writing whether I am at a gallery, at a museum, at a coffee house, at a shrine, at a library, at a theatre, or at a park. And I never forget the place where I read a certain book. I read Zorba the Greek near the bamboo in the Arboretum. I read Hermann Hesse at the Muijiza Theatre. I read Oscar Wilde in the Christian Science Reading Room. I read William Blake's *Songs of Innocence* in a church and his *Songs of Experience* in a coffee house.

"The book and the setting can match or contrast. It does not matter. The important thing is that when I look up from the book, I ideate.

"Ahh, it was grand when the verbs from Zorba, took wing and perched in that swaying bamboo. And it was equally grand when the adjectives in Oscar Wilde leapt from the page and jumped about that bust of Mary Baker Eddy. What daring and original ideas I had. My heart was racing the whole time.

"Ahh… When you really know how to read! Suddenly the patterns of clouds are readable, the boles of the tall cedars are readable, the colors on blouses and shirts in the lobbies of theatres are readable, the pattern of car traffic in the city streets is readable, the pattern of buildings in the city skyline is readable, the flocks of cranes flying above you are readable, the sidewalk traffic is readable, and all the Nairobians you see there are readable – the city is suddenly readable and beautiful when you look up from the book and see. That's the point of reading books. For the looking up part."

I never heard anyone talk about reading that way. I never heard someone speak with so much enthusiasm on the topic. I did not know how to respond to Lwanga. After a long silence I asked my father if we could leave.

I was not sure if I had understood Lwanga, but for a week I experimented with his reading method. Oh my! What discoveries I made in that week. It was so exciting, more than I could contain. I wanted to tell Lwanga.

It was raining that day, but I went anyway. I ran through the rain to the bookstore. Lwanga was nowhere to be seen so I went to the back of the store where he lived. I toweled myself dry but I was shivering. So I decided to boil water in Lwanga's kettle. Soon I was drinking hot coffee at the kitchen table and writing a note to Lwanga. I wrote,

> Nairobi has enchantments for one who wants to be enchanted. For the person who knows how to read, Nairobi is adorned with precious jewels and exotic charms. Parks with every color in the rainbow on display; libraries with oddities on the same shelf with classics; theatres where Nairobians excel at an old and cherished art form; coffeehouses of fine smelling sweets and bitter rumors; churches and shrines and mosques and temples and synagogues where the giants of our faiths are celebrated; museums with 'Hamed' the giant elephant and 'EAR Steam' the giant locomotive; galleries where nationalities mix to talk about art, and being here right now, just being, and the joy of it. I think I am beginning, just beginning, to read

Nairobi.

Mr. Lwanga, I believe there is more, much more you can teach me about the art of reading. I am therefore requesting you in this note to please consider being my Reading Guide.

P. S. -I have decided to stay in Nairobi.

I didn't know where to put the note. I wanted Lwanga to see it as soon as he walked into the room. I bent down and lifted up one end of a rug and slipped a small portion of the note under it. I left most of the note showing. As I put the rug down I noticed that it was a homemade prayer rug. Lwanga had woven a green ibis in the middle of it. *Strange*, I thought, *that he would want to sit with an ibis while reading his rosary.*

Greenbead Initiation (II)

Agio, Wasomaji, December 22, 1979

I did not hear from Lwanga. He sent no reply letter. It seemed to me there should be a reply letter, something in writing, so I went back to the bookstore. Just before going inside something caught my eye in the display window. It was a big green book. On the cover was printed, *December Book.* I had been uneasy about coming back. I did not want to seem dependent. But that green book reassured me; somehow it would be worth it even if I ended up looking a bit weak, or silly.

"Ahhh ... gio," said Lwanga with great warmth. "Welcome!"

"Thank you," I said. And before I could inquire about the book in the display window, Lwanga had escorted me to a little corner of the bookstore where he sat me down next do a drumtable.

"Here we are," said Lwanga. "This is the Chat Corner."

I caught my breath and looked around. There was a bookshelf

behind Lwanga and a bookshelf behind me. Between us there was a large drumtable. On the table I saw a pot of steaming coffee, two cups, and a plate of fresh *mandazi*[4]. "*Kula*[5]," said Lwanga, as he poured coffee into my cup. "I've been waiting for you."

And so I drank my first cup of coffee in the chat corner with the man who was to teach me lectio. I remember everything we said to each other like it happened yesterday.

"What was Mary doing when the angel Gabriel appeared to her?" he asked.

"I don't know."

"The icons," he said. "Picture her in a chair reading a book."

"Oh."

"What do you think she was reading?" he asked.

"I don't know."

"*Exuberance*," he said.

"What?"

"She was doing lectio on the word, 'Exuberance.'"

"What is lectio?" I responded.

"I thought you'd never ask," said Lwanga. "I'll teach you."

"You will?"

"Yes. Listen, young man. Close your eyes and listen to the word, 'Ex-uber-ance.'"

I closed my eyes and he put an egg into my hand. That made me open my eyes again but the Ibis-Keeper placed his big hands over my eyelids and closed them. "Listen," he said. "And picture what I am saying."

"Ex," he said. "It means out of.

"Uber," he said. "It means up over.

"Ance," he said. "It means flowing.

"Put them together," he said, "and you get 'Out of, Up over, Flowing,' or Exuberance."

I opened my eyes. "I don't get it."

"Okay. Let me put it this way," he said. "Flowing, Up Over,

---

[4] *Mandazi* – Kenyan doughnuts.

[5] *Kula* – Eat.

Out of!" And he stood up, raised both his fists in the air, and popped them open shouting: "Exuberance!"

"I don't get it," I said.

He sat down, shaking his head, and took the egg back. "Tomorrow," he said in a low voice.

"Tomorrow, before sunrise," he continued with eyes closed. "You go to the arboretum."

"And what do you want me to do there?" I asked.

"Just sit. And wait. You'll see," said the Reader's Guide.

Chat Corner

JOYFUL MYSTERIES, ACCORDING TO A YOUNG ARTIST

Nativity (Arboretum, Reader's Guide)

Agio, Wasomaji, December 29, 1979

When I next came into the bookstore, Lwanga noted that my sandals were muddy with highland soil. He asked me what I was doing in the Arboretum before sunrise. I answered, "I went there as you suggested. Let me tell you the story.

"My luck. The stars are out, all sparkling, as the poet says: *Nyota za Mbinguni zilikuwa zikimetameta.*[6] Venus, too, is still visible, immense and sparkling. No moon, just *metameta*[7] stars.

"With aforesaid Venus and two other shining planets a silver halo appears round the tall Himalyan Cypress by the forester's office. Its needles are lit by the stars, and they become green piney candles, each glittering with a Heavenly light.

"A star fire burns 46 billion miles away, and here these little cypress needles glitter. The starlight shines in my face too. Hheewee, a kiss. It feels like a kiss. A big kiss from a big lover. A star kiss.

"Glittering like the needles from toes to fingers, I sit down on an Arboretum bench, dizzy because I feel so well, electric, so connected. I'm a dancer

---

[6] *Nyota za Mbinguni zilikuwa zikimetameta* - All the stars of Heaven were sparkling.
[7] *Metameta* – Sparkling.

whirling in the big dance; and, dear me, I feel something more – something embarrassing, sounding too sentimental – I feel MERRY! That's the best adjective for it. MERRY!

"And I say to myself, life does not get better than this. I can stay contented the rest of my life on this park bench.

"Then comes the excess.

"'An ibis,' I whisper.

"I'm happy enough I think. Why more?

"Yet the universe behaves that way. A great lover. A lover who lifts one beyond the pleasure boundary, into an ecstasy overpassing ecstasy.

"'Oohh. Oh, my, that's already good enough,' I whisper to the park bench, clutching the slats of it, but the universe lifts me higher.

"'You excessive, illimitable lover,' I say to the gorgeous heavenlies. 'You've never enough. Just go ahead then. Finish me.'

"I should have known this would happen when I saw the shining planets halo the cypress. There's always a hint.

"'An ibis!' I whisper again.

"A mother ibis. She nests in the branches of the haloed cypress. Her green eyes are wide open. And gosh, she looks merry too. Her egg has just hatched.

"'Stay merry, avian mother," I whisper.

"Then I hear the eggshell, spent in cracking open, say to its former tenant,

'Happy Hatch-Day, Homely Hatchling.'

"Am I that eggshell? Or outside it?

"Or, am I the eggshell that I am outside of?

"Yes, that's what's going on. My ecstasy is an egg and it cracked. So I'm outside ecstasy, beyond it, ecstatic of ecstasy.

"And I expect this ecstatic ecstasy may also crack.

"Oh, *Exuberance*!...

"I am not complaining but I am so little, how can the universe imagine that I can endure its exuberance? Containing the uncontainable will crack me and crack me continuously, until I am no more than powder.

"For two or three hours I sit on the park bench watching the cypress and the ibises. Then, with the sun at *saa tatu*,[8] I stand up, cypress still glittering, and walk slowly out of the park.

"Has such a thing ever happened to you?" I asked Lwanga after relating to him the story of my second birth.

"Often," answered Lwanga, sipping his morning tea.

"Egg," I said. "Incredible enough. Quite enough. But egg within egg, coming out and coming out, the uncontainable ever coming out. This cracking hatchling force. Is any greater?"

Lwanga looked at me. "None greater. You cannot stop hatching. You cannot go back into any of the broken shells. You are already too big the instant you come out. But why go back? Soon you'll crack again and be outside that self too. Let the

_____

[8] *Saa tatu* – 9 A.M.

cracking force crack you. You cannot stop it. You'll never put Humpty Dumpty back together again. Humpty Dumpty is already another person before you try."

Suddenly I was very hungry and stuffed my mouth with marmalade toast. But then an important question came to me, so I swallowed hard and fast to ask, "What of the sound?"

"The Wolof in West Africa," Lwanga replied, "have a word in their language for the sound an egg makes when it hatches. They say this sound was the primal sound, the word for all that is."

"*Kraaack!* The primal sound," I laughed. "The word for all that is."

"And is to be," said Lwanga with his eyes closed. "The inexorable cracking-hatchling-force of the uncontainable."

Annunciation: How the Paint Brush Chose Me

Agio, Wasomaji, January 5, 1980

"Why Luke?" I asked.

"His is the most Marian Gospel according to friends of mine who are painters," said Lwanga.

"He is?"

"We know Luke was a painter," said Lwanga. "Readers of Luke say that his Gospel has more images in it, more pictures to contemplate."

"Why not Mark?" I asked.

"Oh no," said Lwanga. "Mark writes about Jesus much differently. The reader of Mark often sees the word 'immediately.' Jesus immediately goes here or goes there; immediately does this or does that. Jesus is very busy, almost frantic. There is so little time to get his work done. Mark is an action film like *Rambo*."

"What analogies come to mind when you think of Luke?" I asked.

"The Paintings of the French Impressionists," said Lwanga. "Yes," he continued, "Luke makes me think of Monet or

Cezanne."

I asked Lwanga where I should read the Gospel of Luke. He sent me to the arboretum. He told me to read it at high noon. The sunlight of our equatorial home he told me is most exuberant then, almost alive.

Let me tell you what happened. It took place on the last Saturday of January, 1964, several months before my parents died.

I was sitting in the center of a green bench by a Thevetia tree. An older woman came up to me. She told me her name was Naibis and asked if she could sit with me. I nodded, moved over, and made room for her on the bench.

Neither of us spoke during those fifteen minutes of our first meeting. I read Luke. She, well, she seemed... and this sounds odd ... she seemed to cluck. To me, anyway, the sound from her throat was like clucking.

But later when I was back in the chat comer of the bookstore and made the sound for Lwanga, he laughed and said, "You grew up speaking KiSwahili and you didn't recognize the verb prefix, '*Ka*'?"

"Oh!" I said with some embarrassment. "I didn't think of that."

Lwanga went on. "'*Ka*' is the story prefix for picture-verbs, for fiction-verbs; '*Ka*'' helps us suspend disbelief so that we can enjoy the narration of a fable or tale."

"Oh my. I never thought of '*Ka*' quite that way."

"Of course," said Lwanga. "'*Ka*' is an essential tool in the art of language; it is to the story writer what a brush is to the painter."

"Why did the woman – I think she said her name was Naibis – cluck '*Ka*' while I was reading the Gospel of Luke?"

"Perhaps," Lwanga said, "it was to help you read the life of Jesus."

"Well," I said, "I didn't get far."

"Oh?"

"I found myself doing lectio on the words of Gabriel to Mary, '*Gratia Plena.*' The angel called her 'Grace-Full.'"

"Yes," said Lwanga. "The Gospel of Luke is the only one which features the Annunciation to Mary. When reading Luke, I have often asked myself how many women prior to Mary did the angel visit? The angel's message is always the same, *'Gratia Plena'* but others perhaps refused to accept the salutation. 'Who me? I'm not Grace-Full, beautiful.'"

"But Mary accepted the greeting," I said.

"Yes," said Lwanga. "She agreed with the angel. She recognized in herself the beauty hailed by the angel. And that is why she was able to point it out to others. I can see her greeting friends that way, *'Gratia Plena.'* I can see her greeting every creature she encountered that way, 'You are Grace-Full, beautiful.'"

"Is that why Luke liked to write about her?"

"Yes," said Lwanga. "She is a guide to painters, writers, sculptors, dancers, musicians and everyone who engages in art because she gives them eyes for grace, eyes for exuberance."

While Lwanga was talking about eyes I felt a tingling in my hands. And my hands didn't stop shaking until Lwanga gave me a paintbrush to hold.

You might laugh at me when I say it. But it seemed then that the paintbrush chose me. I still don't know what Lwanga was doing with a paintbrush that day at the chat corner.

But the paintbrush appeared, right then, when my fingers were itching for it, and, just as he was giving it to me, I heard a bird clucking in the loft above the chat corner. It sounded to me like it said "*Ka.*"

Temple Presentation

Agio, Wasomaji, January 12, 1980

"Temple Presentation," Lwanga said.

"Two of the Joyful Mysteries involve Temple. Why?" I asked Lwanga.

"'Temple' is related to the word 'Time.'"

"So?"

"So if you understand time you enter the joy... What do you think of the African who said to the hurried unhappy Englishman, 'You have watches, we have time?'"

"He was making an excuse for being late."

"Maybe," laughed Lwanga, "but I think he was also speaking about the mystery of time. Europeans want to save time. Africans want to create it. If a guest comes, even though I had other plans for the day, I drop the plans, and create time. This, Agio, is a great power. You and I are not slaves to time. Watches only measure time; temple people create it."

Then I asked, "What has this to do with my vocation?"

Lwanga picked up a book by Joseph Campbell and read,

> "... In order to experience what is before him, the artist has mainly to look; and looking, finally, is an unaggressive activity. One does not say to one's eyes, 'Go out and do something to that thing out there.' One looks, looks long, and the world comes in. There is an important Chinese word, *wu-wei*, not doing, the meaning of which is not 'doing nothing,' but 'not forcing.' Things will open up of themselves, according to their nature." [9]

Lwanga closed the book. "Sit. It is the ultimate act of free will. Sit and look long until, of itself, your nature opens. The first thing a creative person must create is time."

---

[9] *The Power of Myth*, Anchor Books, N.Y., 1988.

A Child in the Temple

Agio, Wasomaji, January 26, 1980

Attending classes at the Nairobi Institute of Fine Art in 1969 I got to know other aspiring artists. Some of them were very work-oriented. They could not stroll the city gardens or wander the streets, or stretch out on the park grass. They were too busy making pictures. Pictures that made you nervous.

"Paint in the Temple," Lwanga told me one day.

"What are you talking about?"

"I'm talking about lifestyle."

Lwanga and I were sitting in the chat corner. I had complained about the unleisurely behavior of my classmates. And I knew the topic – leisure – would elicit comments from the Keeper of Thoth[10].

"I have a book for you to read," said Lwanga. "It's called *Leisure, the Basis of Culture*. The author is Josef Pieper."

Lwanga stood up, gracefully. He straightened his back vertebrae by vertebrae, each inch of the way up, as he assumed the vertical position.

I love to watch Lwanga stand up. He never jumps to his feet. Expressions like jump to, spring to, or hurry to would never apply to the way Lwanga gets to his feet. Lwanga takes his time to stack his vertebrae one on top of the other. Some tall people seem embarrassed by the time it takes them to get vertical, and don't take the time to settle themselves straight on their long backbone; they jump up and then walk around bent.

Once on his feet Lwanga moved from the hip. Again, gracefully. The legs were in charge. They led the way. He doesn't walk shoulder first, stooped over, as does a hurried person with a visible load or an invisible load on the back.

---

[10] *Thoth* - Egyptian God of Reading who lived in Ibises. Lwanga kept an Ibis in the third floor loft of his bookstore. He would often visit the loft and sit with the Ibis.

Lwanga is not a burdened person (even if he must carry something); there is something carefree about his locomotion. His steps are bouncy, athletic, spirited, ballet-like. The observer can almost feel the pleasure Lwanga takes in the physical act of walking.

After a few minutes among the green shelves Lwanga returned with Pieper's book. "Here," he said. "Take this to a few Nairobi Temples and seat yourself in the quiet corners of these Temples and read about leisure."

A week later, Lwanga and I were in the chat corner again.

"The Temples made me uncomfortable."

Lwanga tilted his head in a question mark, "Bad architecture? Poor art? Rickety chairs?"

"No, the idea."

"The idea of a temple?"

"The idea of those temples."

"Which did you visit?"

"The one dedicated to Our Lady of Consolata and the one dedicated to Our Lady Help of Christians."

"Great Marian shrines," said Lwanga.

"I'm not a social activist, but the idea of spending money that way in a city of hungry children is grotesque. And if the idea is ugly, the temple itself, regardless of its artistic qualities, is ugly."

"And art for art's sake?" asked Lwanga.

"You are abusing the phrase."

"Okay, you tell me, Agio. What's your idea of temple?"

"The Arboretum," I said.

"And what's temple-y about the Arboretum?"

"Leisure," I said.

"Yes, lllleisure," Lwanga said rolling the 'L' with pleasure. Yes, let's talk about Pieper's book."

"Leisure," I said, "is the basis of culture. From playing around or doing nothing, art is born. Pieper says that even the history of the word shows it to be the basis of culture. Let me read him to you.

> "...For leisure in Greek is *Skola,* in Latin, *Scola,* and in English, School. The word to designate the place where we educate and teach (culture) is derived from a word which means leisure."

"*Scola* designates the place and time for leisure," said Lwanga. "Think of the fifth joyful mystery. Mary finds young Jesus in the Temple. Do you remember those pictures of the boy, age twelve, holding a scroll and standing in front of a group of old bearded men dressed in the heavy robes of temple scribes and they, with rapt attention, hanging on to each word of the fair-face adolescent. Here in this mystery the Temple or *Scola* (they are the same thing) is a time and place of leisure and the basis of a new culture Jesus is creating."

Lwanga, speaking about the basis of Christian culture, gave me a picture of it – Jesus in the Temple, where he has plenty of time and space, a young man at leisure. This made me wonder about my Big Choice to be an artist.

I tap the drumtable rapidly, stop, and look up. "Lwanga, the choice of art as my career, though important, is not as important as the choice of a lifestyle."

Lwanga reaches over and puts his hand on my hand that I am resting on the cow skin drum. "Do you know why your parents named you, 'Agio?'"

"I know that *agio* means leisure in Italian. My father chose the name. He led a Neapolitan life after retiring from the army. He practiced leisure. *La Dolce Vita!* Each day father got out of bed he recreated his life, himself. A truly cultured man. He had no job, no organized way to spend the hours. He browsed in bookstores, limped along through parks on one leg, drank tea with priests and *rishis*, sat in mosques, and churches, played his clarinet, and painted."

"Agio!" Lwanga said my name softly. "Agio. It suggests a lifestyle. How you might live the painter's life."

"And how implies where – to live in an *agio* way I must enter temple space and time."

"Yes, my green friend. You must enter and sit."

"Sit?"

"A Reader sits in the temple: be it a tree park, flower garden, or grassy hill; church, mosque, or bookstore."

"And then what?"

"Nothing much ... A Reader sits and gazes - at the cypress in the woods, at the crèche in the Basilica, at the plumbago in the garden, the widow in the church, the beggar in the mosque, the sky from the grassy hill, or a friend in the bookstore."

"That's the basis of culture?"

"Yes, Agio. Sitting with. That's the basis of culture. Sitting with trees, with bushes, with widows, beggars, dancers, tricksters, clowns, and friends; sitting with, being at your leisure with people, plants and things is how culture begins."

"And that is why I should do it."

"Oh no, never sit because you should. Do it because sitting is a pleasure. As the sitting psalmist sings:

> How lovely your dwelling place, O Lord of Hosts!
> My soul yearns and pines for the courts of the Lord.
> My heart and my flesh cry out for the living God.
> Even the sparrow finds a home, and the [Ibis] a nest in
> which she puts her young -
> Your altars, O Lord of Hosts, my king and my God...
> I had rather one day in your courts than a thousand
> elsewhere.

> *– Psalm 83:2,3,4,11*

Lwanga had been holding my hand the whole time. Now he let go and reached into his pocket. "Here," he said handing me a string of greenbeads. "Use this whenever you sit."

I took the green rosary and fingered the wooden beads. "Is there a green 'ave' I can use with these beads?"

Lwanga took out his string, and sang the song of the first sitter, that loafer, Adam, the inventor of language. We sang it together:

> *Urembo wa*
> *Ulemwengo[11]*
> Thou, Chlorophyll,
> Flow green in me.

Then Lwanga said, "When you finish with that mantra you can use a second mantra.

"It is C...? D...?"

Sorry, Greenbeads. I probably should have skipped the second mantra all together because I can only remember the first letters of the two words of that mantra, C D. Lwanga said I should use the second mantra when I finish with "*Urembo wa, Ulemwengo, Thou Chlorophyll, Flow Green in Me.*"

As I said, maybe I should have skipped the second mantra. What good is C D? But I wanted to give an historical account of all my youthful conversations with Lwanga. I believe that I should relay everything Lwanga said to be fair to you Greenbeads.

Anyway the fact is I never finished with "*Urembo wa Ulemwengo...*" Chlorophyll, the greening agent in all plant life, was more than enough text for me. I've stayed with the mantra given to me in my youth and I give it to all you young greenbeads. You and I are *Urembo wa Ulemwengo*.

---

[11] *Urembo wa Ulemwengo* – Beauty of Creation.

Rama, the Young Doctor

Editors' note:

"Ancestors and Early Years of Rama" was written by Naibis during the period of "Cold War" between Reds and Greens that ensued after the 1979 breakup of the Circle of Readers. It has remained unpublished until now.

The series, "Passion Mysteries, According to a Young Doctor" was written by Rama himself in 1979 after the breakup of the Circle of Readers. This vocation story was published in the Wasomaji in 1979, and was widely circulated among the Redbeads.

RAMA: ANCESTORS AND EARLY YEARS

Rama's great grandfather arrived in Kenya at the beginning of the 20th century when the British colony was laying the line of rail that now extends from Mombasa to Kampala. Like many other Indians, Indra Rama worked with East African Railways for many years. He spent the first decade of the century setting the slippers from Eldoret to Jinja.

Indra's first view in 1901 of the place he would someday call home was not impressive. Nairobi then was just a railhead at the foot of the great escarpment, which separates the eastern savannah from the Rift valley. The settlement consisted of tents and wooden shacks with muddy paths converging on two or three provision stores run by the East Africa Trading Company. Still, Indra made up his mind that once he had earned enough money he would return to Nairobi and start up his own business.

This finally happened in March 1912 when he established a hardware store on Bazaar Street (now Biashara). Thanks to the building frenzy – the administrative capital of British East Africa was at that point being raised out of dust – the Tool and Nail grew and thrived. The store was eventually passed on in 1945 to Indra's only child, Sita, the mother of our Rama.

A woman inheriting a hardware business made the story of the Indra Ramas a little different than that of other Indian families in Kenya. But something happened in 1938 that made a much greater difference.

Nairobi then was not the cosmopolitan city it has become. There was very little social mixing among the various Asian communities – the Hindus, the Sikhs, the Ismailis, the Goans, the Jains, the Sunnis – each group kept to themselves. Hindu married Hindu; Sikh married Sikh and so on. Social mixing between Asians and Africans was unimaginable.

St. Peter Claver was situated on the border between the Asian neighborhood of Ngara and the African neighborhood of Makogeni. Goans and Africans saw each other at the church on Sunday and always showed each other respect. But they kept their distance ... until Edel Quinn established there in 1938 the first presidium of the Legion of Mary in East Africa. Those first Legion meetings where young Goan Catholics and young African Catholics talked to each other shook Nairobi more than if Mount Longonot had exploded.

Sita Rama, though not a Christian, was intrigued by the unimaginable. One day a Goan girl, shopping in the Tool and Nail, described the Legion meetings to her – that Indians and Africans were talking to each other about life in Nairobi and how to make it better. The next time Sita saw the girl she asked if Miss Quinn would admit a Hindu into the Legion. The Goan made the inquiry and Edel said *"Karibu*[12]*,"* and so Sita began to attend the meetings at St. Peter Claver Church.

Sita was not dissatisfied with Hinduism. She was very devoted to Sri Ram and Sita and Lakshman. She loved to read about these heroes in the Ramayana. That she eventually became a Christian was not, as she saw it, a falling away from Hinduism. It was rather a completion of her faith. She ardently believed in the better world Sri Ram fought to achieve.

Those first Legionnaires did strive to make the world better. Every week at Legion meetings they reported on deeds they did to achieve what Mary wanted. Some Legionnaires did errands for old people. Others taught the children of railway workers how to read and write. There were even some Legionnaires who wrote articles for the Standard Newspaper giving reasons why Kenya should stay out of the looming war in Europe. The Legionnaires urged each other on to greater sacrifice and service, their motto: *"Et Nos Credidimus Caritati"* – as for us, we have believed in Love.

Miss Quinn, like an avatar of Sri Ram, wanted to drive away evil and suffering and to restore divine humanity. "Realize," she wrote, "that Mary loves us ... let us give ourselves completely to her, to be made all His, to be consumed unceasingly. Let us try to give utterly, in every possible way, without counting the cost, to be spent for Christ ... Mary in me will love Her Son."

The Nairobi elite was uneasy with this new movement. They did not appreciate the zeal of the Legionnaires. All this talk of caritas and sharing gave them the jitters. Other Nairobians, shopkeepers and clerks of a conservative bent, also had their misgivings. They did not like the way Miss Quinn integrated the various races in her new presidium.

At a Legion meeting in August 1939, Sita met a recent émigré to Nairobi, a famous Luo chef. He was twenty-one, two years

---

[12] *Karibu* – Welcome.

older than Sita. Initially the mission of R. G. Marie was all they had in common. By the end of the year they discovered something else they had in common – a fluttering in the stomach whenever their eyes met across the Legion table.

After a January 1940 meeting the handsome chef asked Sita if she would join him for a cup of tea at the kiosk outside the church compound on Haile Salaisse street. This was the beginning of a romance that – after three years and much discussion with families – culminated in an unusual and happy wedding in 1943. Our Rama was Sita's third child; he was born on October 7th 1950.

Rama's early years were shaped by two wars: that of the Mau Mau and that of the Legion. Two wars, yes, two means; but one end. The two means were violence and non-violence. The single end: divine humanity.

While the Mau Mau[13] were making their oaths in the Karura forest, a few miles away, Rama and his family were pledging themselves to "The Mighty She Dressed in Battle Array." It is worth looking in on the scene of this presidium Sita conducted with her children every week.

The dining room table is set for a Legion meeting. The best, starched linen dresses the cedar table; the stiff white cloth is flat against the wood and squared at the corners. Flames jump up and down on the wicks of two beeswax candles sitting in Zambia copper candlesticks at either end of the long table. At the center stands the Vexillum that Miss Quinn gave the Africa-Asia couple on their wedding day. Five children of different ages are seated around the table with father at one end and mother at the other. Mother rises and addresses the family.

"My fellow Legionnaires we meet once again to discuss our service to Queen Mary; our victories and our near victories. Let us begin." The father and children rise and say a prayer to the Holy Spirit, then they sit and read five decades of the rosary. After this the oldest child reads from Butler's "Lives of the Saints." The next

---

[13] *Mau Mau* - Kenyan Freedom Fighters who battled the British army.

oldest child then reads the minutes from the last meeting. Each member of the presidium then gives a report of his or her work that week.

"I did my house chores and also the house chores of baby sister because she has the flu." Sita slowly nods her head in solemn approval.

"I helped mother and grandfather with stock keeping at the Tool and Nail." Sita nods.

"I carried the lame boy in my class to the dispensary to collect medicine." Sita nods.

"I washed the laundry of the old widow at the end of our street." Sita nods.

"I changed Tony's nappies." Sita nods but not with full solemnity, smile lines are cracking near her eyes.

Now father begins the Catena prayer. "Who is She...?" he intones. Then Sita gives the Allocutio, this week she dwells on the seven corporal works of mercy. The treasurer makes his report. Finally, Sita gives a work assignment to each Legionnaire for the coming week. To end the meeting the members hold hands, as Sita leads her little presidium in singing the Lourdes Magnificat.

Let's step away from the scene now. It is clear from our time with this presidium that Rama was engaged in the *Nova Bellum*[14] of the Legion Queen. It is however an unfortunate fact (in this hope sick world) that zeal of whatever kind, violent or non-violent, is a target for the cynic. One day after school Brother Polycarp, an English Augustinian, questioned Rama.

"Say there, Master Rama, stay, I want a word with you."

The boy sets down his bundle of books, "Yes, sir."

Brother Polycarp rubs his chin and asks, "What is that pin you are wearing?"

Rama answers with pride, "It is the Legion emblem."

Brother Polycarp laughs, "Well, well, Her Majesty's Navy has a new Jack Tar."

---

[14] *Nova Bellum* - New Wars.

Rama shakes his head, "Excuse me sir?"

The Brother leans against his desk. "You are a seaman bound for the island of disappointment, lad." Rama's face screws up into a question mark.

"Yes, bitter disappointment. I'm warning you. You'll fight, just like these bloody Mau Mau, and you'll surely lose. In this life and in this world nothing is going to change however much you try. Father Augustine taught us that we are saved by grace. Stick to the sacraments lad. That's all you can do. This Legion work, this activism, it's a pile of rhino crap. Miss Quinn has misled you; she is a dangerous influence on the empire, mixing races, undoing the social structure. And besides you're no mariner, you're no fighter, little boy. Don't get hurt my starry-eyed landlubber. When your boat is shelled, full of holes, and shipping water and you find yourself sinking, remember my words, you would-be sailor." Brother Polycarp stood up, moved away from the desk over to the window. With his back to the boy, he said, "Go home now, and take off that silly emblem. You're no Legionnaire. And our Blessed Mother is no Warrior Queen."

Never before in his life had an adult spoken to Rama in such a way. The diction, the vocabulary, were over his head. Rama understood very little of what Brother Polycarp had said except for one thing – Legionnaires would never win their war. This thought threw Rama into a panic. He ran home from school that day and was very quiet at the next family presidium. When it was over he took a walk down Biashara Street to Jevanjee Garden and sat down on a park bench. Suddenly from out of nowhere a sacred Ibis landed ten yards from the bench and started walking toward him. It made no sound. It kept coming closer. And then up it jumped onto the bench. Rama knew little about birds then. He didn't know this was an ibis. Was it looking for food? Rama pulled from his pocket crumbs of a broken biscuit. The Ibis spread its wings as if to cover him. Or maybe it wanted to clutch him and carry him off? The Ibis closed its wings and sat down staring at the boy. There they were, the two of them, the Ibis and the boy, sitting on a bench, darting questions at each other with their eyes.

The Ibis made a sound, like a person, but it seemed impossible to Rama. And from its mouth the Ibis regurgitated a slip of paper that fell onto the park bench. The bird stood up then, made that almost human sound again, and with a ruffle of feathers flew away.

The address of Reader's Guide was printed on the paper. The boy went there the next day. Look at him. He is walking down the sidewalk, head down with the address in hand. He suddenly stops. Something in the corner of his right eye: the color red. He turns his head. It is a display window of books. In the center is the March Book. Young Rama senses that he has found the place where he can find and read himself.

The young legionnaire and Lwanga, the storeowner, quickly became friends. But it was several weeks before Rama would finally raise the question with Lwanga about justice's chances of winning the war.

I Am Rama, Leader of the Redbeads

Rama, Wasomaji, July 2, 1979

Hello. I am Rama, Leader of the Redbeads.

That is the way I like to introduce myself. I am, you see, a perfect personification of Redbeadism. My followers also call me:

Doctor
Fighter
Knight
Warrior
Zealot

I am on the short side, as you know. I weigh less than forty kilos. But don't let me catch you cheating the poor. I have a terrible temper. I'll bite off your head.

I don't dress like other doctors. I'm disheveled in appearance.

Some of you have even mistaken me for a street person. Thank you. I don't bother with fancy clothes. I've got other things on my mind.

Jesus, for me, is a rebel and reformer.

I am very devoted to the sorrowful mysteries. I call them the passion mysteries. These five mysteries are about the great passion of Jesus, a passion for justice. The red beads describe for us the martyr's end; the kind of death Jesus suffered on Calvary.

My name is Rama. I love my name. In the Hindu religion Rama was the Great Warrior who battled injustice and all sorts of evils. He was a passionate hero, a champion of the oppressed. I am Rama, leader of the Redbeads. We will overcome injustice even if it means dying as Jesus died.

Many of you have asked me, "How did you discover your vocation to be a doctor?" Others have asked me, "How did you discover your vocation to be our leader?"

You can read the answer to these questions in the next few issues of the *Wasomaji*. They will feature in serial form both my vocation story, as well as my series based on the rosary that tells how I became the leader of the Redbeads: "Passion Mysteries According to a Young Doctor."

They will begin to appear in July, the month dedicated to the Precious Blood.

And this year, 1979, July is even more important because we are celebrating the Year of the Child. I hope that many of you consider making a blood donation for children. Come down to Martyrs Blood Bank. You are most welcome.

I hope by the end of this series that Redbeads will better appreciate the station we share with R. G. Marie who, at the foot of the cross, ministered to the crucified.

Redbead Initiation (I)

Rama, Wasomaji, July 9, 1979

The setting for my initiation as a Redbead was the Chat Corner of the Reader's Guide bookstore. The year was 1963. Here is the chat I had with the wise Reader who became my Guide.

"It's gone, Lwanga," I said, squinting.

"What's gone, Rama?"

Lwanga knew. It was obvious. One look at me and a simpleton could tell what I had lost. Why else would a 13-year-old man be wearing a *Kanzu*[15]? Why was I levitating my bottom an inch from the wicker chair?

"It's gone, Lwanga."

"What's gone, Rama?"

He's playing with me. His eyes are watering with tease. But he shouldn't play with me. This is serious. I'm serious. Can't Lwanga see me? The man in a man's pain, unable to sit, wounded as a man is wounded.

I placed my hand at the front of the Kanzu. Between my index finger and thumb I pinched the *Kanzu* and slowly pulled it away from the wound. "There, that's better."

I slowly let my bottom touch the wicker chair and let out a soft, tremulous, "Ahhhhhh." That should have convinced him.

"What's gone, Rama?"

Immediately I lifted myself up again and emitted a loud operatic, "Yah, Yah, Yah, Ugh!"

Lwanga turned his head away. "So don't tell me."

I let my bottom land definitively, "Ahhhhhhooooowaaaaaahhhhh."

Tease still in his eyes Lwanga said, "Don't tell me if you don't want to."

---

[15] *Kanzu* - A long, loose-fitting, dress-like robe sometimes used by teen-age boys for several weeks after they are circumcized. Normally a Kanzu is worn by adult men when they go to mosque on Fridays.

"Not that I don't want to tell you, Ibisaji[16], I'm forbidden to tell you."

"Why? For what reason?"

"Wait. Let me ask you a question. Are you circumcised?"

"No. I am not."

"That's the reason. If you are not circumcised I can't tell you what happened to my *Rika*[17] under the *Mugumu*[18] tree."

"Okay," he said shrugging his shoulders.

To my dismay Lwanga fell silent. "But I will tell you, Lwanga, because you are my reading guide."

"Thank you for the appointment," he said with a half smile and little bow.

Then in a solemn tone I disclosed the tribal secret. "The *Mganga*[19]," I whispered, "slit either side of the foreskin and pulled the loose flaps back and pinned them together. But it didn't hurt so much - don't tell anyone that part. You see my body was already numb. We were made to stand waist deep in the cold river for a half hour before sunrise. Despite that, after the cut, we still bled. RED is what I remember of the ceremony. Not much else. Red trickling down, red bright-shining on the upper inside of our black thighs."

Lwanga did not seem sufficiently impressed. "So what's gone is a bit of penis blood." He was smiling, satisfied that he had answered his own question.

Immediately I looked around the bookstore to see if anyone heard him say that body part. "Please, Lwanga, lower your voice. You still don't get it. Come closer, I don't want to shout."

Lwanga leaned toward the drumtable and cupped his hand to his ear and with a stage-whisper asked, "Tell me, Rama, what's gone?"

---

[16] *Ibisaji* – Keeper of Ibises.

[17] *Rika* – A circle of agemates bonded to each other because they were initiated into manhood at the same time.

[18] *Mugumu* – Sacred fig tree of the Kikuyus.

[19] *Mganga* – The holy man, the circumciser.

"My female soul!" I said, hitting the drumtable with my fist.

"Your what?"

"My female soul," I repeated. "A boy is born with two souls and circumcision cuts away the female one. You don't know that? You should know that, Ibisaji."

I didn't want to say it. I knew it would cause him pain. "Lwanga, listen."

"Speak."

"I must leave the circle of Readers."

"But, why?"

"Because the female soul in me is gone, cut away. I no longer have the spirit of R. G. Marie."

Lwanga wrinkled his brow and raised his left eyebrow. "Are you stating a fact or asking a question?"

"Well," I hesitated, "it's a question."

"Put it plainly then."

"Can I be both ... militant and Marian?"

A smile relaxed his forehead. "Militant? You want to join the Mau Mau now." He sat back and folded his arms. "Rama, hasn't anyone told you that Kenya has its *Uhuru*[20]? The Mau Mau have come out of the forest."

I wasn't smiling. Why couldn't Lwanga be serious? "That's not what I'm saying. I know we've got *Uhuru*. In fact, my Rika is called '*Uhuru*' because we are circumcised in 1963.[21] I'm not a Mau Mau. What I'm saying, Lwanga, is that I am a warrior."

"A warrior?"

"Yes, a non-violent warrior, and I'm looking for a suitable spirituality. Something more masculine than Marian. Something soldier-like. Jesuit, perhaps."

"You want to be a Jesuit?"

"As a matter of fact, I'm talking to one of their recruiters. He uses militant analogies and mascu..."

---

[20] *Uhuru* – Freedom.
[21] *1963* – The year Kenya attained its independence.

"Cut, cut! Stop there. There is something you don't know about R. G. Marie."

"What's that?"

Lwanga stood up. I gazed. I loved watching Lwanga move. He raises himself gracefully, giraffe-like, maybe because he is long-limbed, long-necked. Standing, Lwanga removed his sweater and opened three buttons on his red jersey. The contrast of red cotton and black chest reminded me of Rika blood drops on black thighs. I wondered what Lwanga might have looked like if he were with me under the *Mugumu*. Lwanga belonged to another Rika though. He was twenty-six. I was thirteen.

Ibisaji walked to the bookshelf. He reached for and fingered various books, like a giraffe nibbling among leaves. Taking down a book his hairless arms muscled up at the bicep. As he bent his head forward to read the title of the book I saw the back of his neck – clean-shaven, smooth, and dark-warm, earth at nightfall.

"Ah, here it is."

With his longest finger Lwanga stroked the book at its binding. "This is what I wanted."

He handed me the red-jacketed book and said, "Read the title."

"Edel Quinn, Heroine of the Apostolate."

"Keep it a week. Come back then and we'll talk."

"Thanks," I said. "My parents wanted me to read this; now, I want to."

I stood up slowly, ever so slowly, pulled out my *Kanzu* at the groin, and exited groaning and squinting.

Redbead Initiation (II)

Rama, Wasomaji, July 16, 1979

A week after my circumcision I walked into the bookstore with a canvas. At the chat corner I leaned the painting against the wall. Seeing me enter, Lwanga gave a little bow to the customer he was serving, excused himself and came to me.

"Did you read it?"

"Yes. I painted it too."

"Show me," he said.

I turned the picture around.

Lwanga knelt near the painting and pointed at each shade of red. "Sixteen," he said. "And there's not only flame in her heart, there's tongues of flame in every part of her body."

Lwanga looked up at me and then at the painting, pointing again. "This fire in her hands is like our best soil. This fire in her mantle is like the Rift Valley dawn. This red in her throat is the fire of the dragon flower. This red in her heart is the fire of Rika blood."

Ibisaji stood up and took in the painting as a whole. "The baby she is holding could be any child. Not distinct enough to be called Kikuyu, or Maasai, or Mzungu, or Indian. R. G. Marie is mother of all."

I pointed to the eyes, "Do you see the fire here, the iris redness?"

"Yes, explain it to me," said Lwanga.

"R. G. is staring down something that threatens the child... The Terrible. That is her name. She frightens the tyrant."

"Terrible who?" asked Lwanga.

"She, Terrible, an army in battle array."

"Ah, you did read Edel Quinn."

"Her favorite phrase for R. G., out of the Song of Solomon. To Edel and her Legion, Our Lady is a warrior queen. You've shown me the way, Lwanga."

PASSION MYSTERIES ACCORDING TO A YOUNG DOCTOR

Descent of Sophia, 1963

Rama, Wasomaji, July 23, 1979

"Where?"

"Do you know the arboretum?"

"Yes."

"Go there. Sit on a park bench and wait."

"For what?"

"Zeal."

"But how is..."

Lwanga held a finger to his lips and shooed me out the door with his other hand.

After waiting on the park bench for forty minutes, as I was about to leave, it came.

A bird. It circled above the trees. Effortlessly. Then it dipped, sharply. Down near to me, so close I could count individual feathers. Up again it went. Even higher above the trees, circling. Then once more it dipped, sharply. It came near to me, then flew slowly ahead of me, skirting the level path, and calling me, "Raaa Ma, Raaa Ma, Raaa Ma." I followed this trailblazer a few meters. Then it lifted itself with three powerful strokes of its giant wings. Up and up it ascended, over the trees and away toward the city, calling, "*Anga, anga, anga*[22]."

When I told Lwanga of the incident, he wanted me to describe the bird. "Did it look like mine?" he asked.

But I couldn't say. I had not observed its features in detail.

"Go back, Rama. Wait for that bird. This time note its features. Write down what you see."

The next day I bounded through the door, running into the

---

[22] *Anga* – Brightness or light.

middle of the shelves of books. Lwanga was with a customer, but I pushed my way between them. I held out the notebook, still panting, and said, "Read this."

Lwanga read aloud:

"Large body, about 30 inches long. White plumage. Black ornamental feathers on the lower back. Wide wingspan. A crane's neck. Long legs. The head and neck are bare of feathers. The exposed skin is black. Long single beak, turned in. Quiet. Unafraid. Stares at things as if thinking."

Lwanga looked up from the notebook. "Rama, you saw a Sacred Ibis. We need to talk. Go to the chat corner. I'll join you in a moment."

After finishing with the customer, Lwanga came. He sat down by the drumtable, pushed his chair over until it touched mine, and said, "Do you know that at Great Zimbabwe the priests of Hungwe interpreted the cries of the Fish Eagle to the King of the Karana? Soapstone carvings of these *Shirit ya Mwari* still perch on the turrets of the palace."

"But I saw an ibis you said."

"Right. It's a bird with a message for you."

"What should I do?"

"Return to the arboretum," he said. "If you see the Ibis, say, 'Perch, your servant is listening.'"

I tapped the drumtable and laughed. "This is really getting straaaaange." I shook my head, "So tell me Lwanga, if the bird does perch, what do I do then?"

"You bring me whatever the Ibis gives you."

The following day I strolled into the bookstore waving a feather. I was laughing. "See what it left me? The Ibis did perch. And then flew away. I found this under the tree. Sorry, Lwanga." I tossed the feather into the trash basket.

Lwanga retrieved the feather and told me to take a seat. He put the feather on the drum next to a large picture book. Then he picked up the book. I could see the title: *Birds of Africa*. He started to read:

"Sacred Ibis, Threskiornis Aethiopica... The ancient

Egyptians regarded this ibis as sacred and were responsible for its popular name. The bird was depicted on many murals and frequently mummified specimens have been discovered in tombs. It was revered as the embodiment of Thoth, the god of wisdom, the scribe of the gods and guide of readers."

After Lwanga finished reading I said, "So what?"

Lwanga held out the feather. "I want to do a little experiment with this feather, if you agree."

"Experiment?"

"I'd like to climb the book stack ladder to the second level of shelves and drop this feather. Whatever book it lands near, you must read."

I tapped the drum, intrigued. "Sure," I said, and chuckled. "What a way to choose a career."

Lwanga heard me and said, "Zeal has found you and it is going to use you."

Ibisaji climbed up the stack ladder and from the top he yelled down, "Here goes." Then he dropped the Ibis feather. It floated gently down, made a half circle, and landed in the far left corner of the bookstore. Both hands in my pockets, fearful, I walked slowly over to the feather. I bent over, shook my head, and shouted up to Lwanga, "It's landed near your twelve volume set of the Medical Encyclopedia."

Slaughter of the Innocents, 1974

Rama, Wasomaji, July 30, 1979

After four years of medical study I began my residency at Kenyatta National Hospital. There I encountered many sorrows.

"An old doctor," I said leaning toward the drumtable, "told me how he handles death."

"How?" asked Lwanga, putting a hand to his chin.

"This old doctor told me that after his first year of practice he had made an estimate of how many children in his care would die in a year. He called this his average. He was working to improve his average. He stopped thinking of this or that particular child. He made it into a game. Just to stay interested. Other than that he was resigned. 'That's the key to sanity in this profession' he told me. 'Resign yourself to the fact that children also die.'"

Lwanga got up and stood by the window. He put his right hand on the back of his neck. But he didn't hide the handsome curve of his head. I thought about the human skull. How it is used in horror movies as a symbol for things grim and morbid. Unfairly used in my opinion. The skull is a beautiful part of human anatomy, with its lobes and crevices each having a purpose. Nothing is more important to intelligent life. This wired globe. This moon shaped light bulb in the socket of the body. It is cratered by meteors of thought that impact its inside surface. For millennia, insights have creviced the moon-skull and given it that human distinction. Still gazing at the exquisite form of Lwanga's head, I wondered which insights had made him so beautiful.

Lwanga turned toward me and said, "When I taught primary school for a year, I remember speaking with an older teacher who told me that whenever one of his students died it seemed to him that death was invented that day, that moment. Death for him was always something unexpected as if death was not meant to be and yet it happens. This older teacher told me that he could never resign himself to the death of children. He even took a vow that he would always treat a child's death as something artificial, a contrivance, not due, unfair."

Ward 22 was my first residency post. It is where children suffering from *kwashiokor* and *marasmus*[23] are treated. There are hundreds of children in this ward. They come from Kibera, Mathare, Mukuru, Kawangware, Kangemi, Korogocho. Though born in these shantytowns, they are properly nourished with breast milk until two or so. That's when their demise begins. Kibera, Mathare and such places haven't the wherewithal to wean their

---

[23] *Kwashiokor* and *marasmus* – Two kinds of severe malnutrition.

babies. Mothers of the shanties can't afford KCS[24] milk or the uji[25] or the fruits.

I saw Ward 22 as a net that catches the children of the shanties. They fall from their mother's breast. From the city. And they are caught by the net of Ward 22. I wish it were a better net. More tightly woven, because some children fall through it and away into death.

One such child, Wambui, appeared in the net when I was on duty. She was from Kibera. She suffered with *marasmus*. Poor weaning. Hadn't tasted milk since the mother's. The lack had wasted Wambui. Her body weight was half what it should have been. She didn't cry though. She was listless. We put her on intravenous drip. We gave her vitamins and protein. Wambui gained weight, recovered. After a month she was released. Three months later Wambui was back. This time she was even thinner. Her breathing was irregular. So, too, her treatment. The drips, the feeds, the poems. We monitored her closely. I stayed up at night with Wambui. When I held her and recited Swahili nursery rhymes, it calmed her. She would smile. But the drips and the poems didn't work.

In the chat corner the next day I said, "Rachel is weeping for her children and is not going to be consoled."

Lwanga was silent and shut his eyes as I talked.

"You know Albert Camus wanted to become a believer, but never could because of the second chapter of St. Mathew."

"The Massacre of the Innocents," Lwanga said with his eyes still closed.

I nodded. I didn't want to speak. Lwanga opened his eyes. "And you, Rama, what do you feel when a child dies of *marasmus* in Ward 22. I mean at the moment of death."

Words gushed out of me then. Words over the silence, water from a broken hydrant, "I feel like smashing the intravenous bottle

---

[24] KCS – Kenya Creamery Service.

[25] *Uji* – Corn meal porridge.

on the floor. I want to kick the bed. I want to scream a big NO. And damn it, I want to give up medicine."

Lwanga said, "The anger is good. Clean. It is a wild bull. It can produce crops – if harnessed."

"Harnessed to what?"

"To medicine."

I didn't get it, and shrugged my shoulders.

"Medicine is your plough but you want to give it up. You think it better to be a raging bull and squander the power anger has created. What a waste," Lwanga said, shaking his head. "All that energy unharnessed."

"I was a doctor. Now I'd rather be a monk or a writer and retire. There are many doctors that have become writers. Take Somerset Maughm, or Boris Pasternak, or St. Luke."

"Let me tell you a story, Rama.

"Pseudo, a prince, went out of his castle on the first day and met sickness. In the castle he was told that such was the lot of mortals in the world. He returned on the second day and met old age. In the castle he was told that such was the lot of mortals in the world. He returned on the third and met death. It was then that Pseudo renounced the world and said he'd never return to it. Thus he achieved Pseudo-Enlightenment."

After telling me this story, Lwanga gave me a red rosary and said, "Use these red beads to read Kenyatta National Hospital. Say: '*Uwezo wa uzazi*[26].' And remember, Rama, when you meet sorrow you will have to choose one of two things: to fight or to flee. Pseudo made his choice. Some think he was a holy man. I don't."

[26] *Uwezo wa uzazi* – Mother Power.

Blood of Delivery, 1975

Rama, Wasomaji, August 4, 1979

My next residency post was the maternity ward. I was responsible for blood transfusions.

Seeking blood donors, I went to Readers' Guide with a painted poster.

"Of course, yes. It'll hang by the front door. Customers will see it there. I'll encourage them to respond. I'm bled every three months and none the worse for it." I handed Lwanga the rolled up poster and thanked him for agreeing to recruit donors. "Books, blood, what's the difference?" he said smiling.

"You've donated plenty of your own blood," I said. "But, me, I never thought much about blood until this assignment. Now that I'm in the maternity ward it's ever on my mind. I've seen what transfusions can do to revive a mother after a difficult delivery."

Lwanga was unrolling the poster as he listened to me. He kept repeating, "Books and blood; books and blood…"

When the poster was fully unrolled Lwanga placed it on the drumtable. "What have we here?"

"It's Mother Jesus," I said, "Lying on the cross. Medieval writers called the cross a birthing table. There Jesus delivered us by his precious blood."

Lwanga scratched his head, "Precious blood, delivery blood. What do you know?"

Work at the maternity ward was interesting. I liked going to the hospital now. I was glad I had not given it up.

I learned all about blood transfusion, about the Wasserman test, and screening out infected blood, about blood identification: Type A, Type B, Type AB, and Type O. I learned about separating red blood cells from plasma. I was especially good at detecting clumps when mixing a sample of the donated blood to a sample of the recipient's blood. Clumps were a message from the recipient that the donor was not welcome. So when this happened, I called off the match. The recipient's blood had to say, "*Karibu*."

After two weeks, I returned to Readers' Guide to ask Lwanga about the response of bookstore customers.

Lwanga invited me to coffee and scones at the drumtable. After pouring my cup, he pulled a piece of paper out of his pocket. He held it in his hand and gave me his report:

"Readers of gothic who-done-it, two.
Readers of travel books, none.
Readers of spiritual books, none.
Readers of comic books, three.
Readers of sports books, none.
Readers of cookbooks, ten.
And I also gave."

"Not bad," I said, "that's fourteen pints of blood."

"You think fourteen in two weeks is not bad? But I see seventy people come through that door every day," said Lwanga.

He was disappointed in his customers. It bothered me to see him sad. I offered an excuse for them, "Maybe people overvalue the drops of their blood," I said.

"And undervalue the blood of mothers."

"What do you mean, Lwanga?"

"Take the ward you're in now. Think of the amount of blood shed there in a year's time and over a decade and a score of years. Think of the amount of blood shed in all maternities and home deliveries in this country. Think of the hundreds of gallons of blood shed to give birth on this continent; think of the thousands of gallons shed for the children of the world. Imagine that donation. It's not in any blood bank savings account, it's humanity's current account. And it bothers me that few people know that or value it."

"Women's un-precious blood."

"It seems," said Lwanga. "But," he added, "It was not always un-precious. Last century devotion to the blood of R. G. Marie was quite popular in Italy. A major study was written on the maternal blood: '*Del Sangue Purissimo E Virginale della Madre*

de Dio Maria.' But it was placed on the index of forbidden books
by the Holy Office in January 1875 and the devotion was banned."

Lwanga looked at my poster. "Do you think Jesus would ban
a devotion to the blood of the one who shed it for him?"

I shook my head.

"Well," said Lwanga, "then I propose we begin a devotion to
the Blood of Delivery. If blood misspilt for the nation has been
glorified in wars of the 20th century, why not, in the 21st, glorify
blood spilt to birth children?"

Transfailurization, 1976

Rama, Wasomaji, August 11, 1979

My final residency post was the postnatal clinic. There I
immunized infants against tuberculosis, diphtheria, whooping
cough, tetanus, polio, and measles. I liked this more than curative
medicine. Immunology attracted me and I was inclined to make it
my field of specialization. One day I went to Lwanga to get his
advice.

"Why be an immunologist?" said Lwanga. He put the milk
pitcher and two glasses on the drumtable and sat down.

"An immunologist," I said, "makes the blood of children
resistant to bacteria and virus. The vaccine I administer calls up
the reservists already in the blood and makes them warriors. And
each specific vaccine alerts a specific warrior to the peculiar threat
of a specific enemy. My immunizing needle is the reveille bugle
to these various warriors:"

> *Amkeni, amkeni, amkeni,*
> Kuna kifua kikuu mwilini,
> Mwendeni, mkifukuzeni.[27]

---

[27] *Amkeni...* – Up! Up! Up! / There's TB in the body, / Go! Sweep it away!

"The braves mobilize the instant they hear my fight song."

Lwanga laughed. "Well, it sounds like you have the missiology of immunology figured out."

"And the soteriology too."

"Oh?"

"The soteriology of transfailurization."

"Huh?"

"You see, Lwanga, the dead or injured germ is used in a vaccine. The body receives a disease in order to be free of disease. Just like the crucified one took sin into himself and transfailurized it, God tricks evil and uses it to defeat evil."

"You've been thinking a lot about this career, Rama. Tell me, have you also a Mariology of Immunology?"

Lwanga poured milk into the two glasses. He was smiling. He enjoyed discussing odd-ologies. In Catholicism, he once told me, there are many -ologies. The Catholic Church is universal. Or in other words, according to Lwanga, the roof of the Catholic Church is the sky. And it covers a spectrum of colors.

Lwanga himself is the most catholic (universal) human I've ever met. This thought occurs to me as he hands me a glass of milk. Look at him. He is wearing a bead necklace of many colors. I see red of course. But it also has a generous portion of green beads, yellow beads, blue beads, and orange beads. I so enjoy gazing at Lwanga. He is the most interesting book in the store. And every day he sports a different book jacket. Today Lwanga is wearing a *kofia*[28] with constellations sewn into it. I also see a small seashell hanging in the lobe of his left ear. The rainbow around his neck, the constellation on his head, the ocean at his ear, all gives Lwanga a very catholic appearance. (But, Redbeads, we must not become this catholic. We must remember the priority of red.)

After taking a sip of the milk I say, "You're asking if there is

---

[28] *Kofia* – hat.

a Mariology of Immunology. Well, of course there is. It may sound strange to you though."

"Go ahead," said the catholic Ibisaji, "Try me."

"Okay, think of breast milk. It is the only food produced by love."

"True," said Lwanga.

"Men do not have the bosoms women have."

"True again," said Lwanga rubbing his chest.

"But men can give children elements of breast milk."

"Such as antibodies," said Lwanga smiling.

"Precisely." I looked at my hand and touched the milk pitcher. "An immunologist, you might say, is another breast for the child. My great-grandfather, a Hindu, used to boast of his third eye. We, Redbeads, can boast of our third breast."

Lwanga slapped his knee and laughed, "You claimed your female soul was cut away at circumcision, now you boast of a maternal organ."

I took my hand from the milk pitcher. "I was wrong, Lwanga. I do not have a female soul, but I do have a female organ. My breast feeds a child with protection against diphtheria, whooping cough, tetanus, and polio at six weeks, ten weeks, and fourteen weeks. My breast feeds a child with protection against measles at nine months."

"So you're going to use *uzazi*[29] zeal through immunology."

I looked at my hands again and then at Lwanga. "Someone once told me zeal would use me."

Lwanga winked, nodded his head, said "Amen," and poured me another glass of milk.

---

[29] *Uzazi* – Motherhood or fatherhood.

Warrior Passion, 1976

Rama, Wasomaji, August, 18, 1979

The reading space in my second story flat is small. It's a corner of my bedroom having two windows that touch at a right angle. They are big windows facing the skyline of Nairobi. My street is called Lower Hill. It is on a hundred meter rise above city center, and about a fifty-meter drop from Kenyatta National Hospital.

Out of the windows of my reading space I can see the coffee cup restaurant on top of Kenyatta Conference Center. I can also see the Empire Hotel on Kenyatta Avenue and the roof of the New Stanley Hotel farther down the Avenue. I can hear the faint noise of traffic on Uhuru Highway, but I can't see it because of a copse of eucalyptus that grows between Lower Hill and city center.

Sitting in my reading chair with *Drumtaps* on my lap I look up through the glass at my tall neighbors. I repeat Whitman's words to those eucalyptus:

> Beat! Beat! drums! ---- blow bugles! blow!
> Make no parley ---- stop for no expostulation,
> Mind not the timid ---- mind not the weepers or prayers,
> Mind not the old man beseeching the young man...
> So strong you thump O terrible drums ----
> So loud you bugles blow.

I stand up and put Whitman back on the bookshelf. The sun's rays are now touching all my titles. I gaze at them as one would the faces of comrades on the eve of battle.

Ramayana by Rajaji
The Plague by Albert Camus
Wretched of the Earth by Franz Fanon
African Socialism by Leopold Senghor
The Future of Man by Teillhard de Chardin
Facing Mount Kenya by Jomo Kenyatta

Don Quixote by Miguel Cervantes
Liberation Theology by Gustavo Gutierrez
The Last Temptation of Christ by Nikos Kazantzakis
The Brothers Karamazov by Feodor Dostoevsky
A Commentary on the Gospel of Mark

Lwanga lent me these books during my residency year at
KNH. Now I must return them to him. The boxes are on my bed,
and soon, books in boxes, and boxes in the gardener's
wheelbarrow, will be rolling into Readers' Guide.

But with morning sunshine coming through my windows
irradiating the books, I delay packing for a moment, and just stand
back and lectio the bookshelf. How pleasant to gaze at books
leaning against each other on a shelf. It feels good to be near them.
Not as possessions, but as friends. I imagine myself on the shelf
leaning on my friends.

After a while I go to the bed, pick up three boxes, and carry
them with one hand to the reading space. As I pack each book I
hold the author in both hands. "Good-bye, Ngugi wa Thiongo,
Lord Byron, Jeremiah the Prophet, Karl Marx, Mark the
Evangelist, Mahatma Ghandi, Julius Nyerere, Moses, Nelson
Mandela, Oscar Romero, Martin Luther King, Tom Mboya,
Albert Schweitzer."

Each person reminds me of a place. Not the home of the author
or the setting of the book but the spot in Nairobi where I read that
book, KNH Casualty, Afya House, The City Morgue, Holy Trinity
Church Kariobangi, St. John Korogocho, St. Theresa Church
Eastleigh, Jamia Mosque Center City, Khoja Mosque Moi
Avenue, Brahmin Temple Ngara, St. Mary Cemetery at the grave
of Edel Quinn, Freedom Fighter Exhibit at the National Museum.

Places. The color and sound and smell of the places I've read,
came back to me as I held each book. I remembered the context
with the text.

After I had packed all the boxes, I sat down in my reading
chair and took out my red beads. I looked at the boxes of books
and the near-empty bookshelves. In desperation I looked around

the room for companionship. I set my eyes on the pictures hanging on the wall. There was an icon of Joan of Arc, a painting of Anaawarita[30], a drawing of Bhakita[31], a drawing of Donna Beatrice[32], a photo of Dorothy Day, a painting of Delacroix of Liberté Storming the Barricade, an icon of Theresa of Avila, a photo of the former mayor of Nairobi, Margaret Kenyatta, and a photo of the Statue of Liberty. What did they all have in common? They were all women with great animus. I then began to say Mary's mantra: "*uwezo wa uzazi*[33]."

As I fingered the beads and looked at my collection of amazons, I thought of Lwanga. Why do I have these thoughts about him? Then it came to me. He was a red Marian. He was a male amazon. He was what R. G. Marie would be like if she were a man.

I got up and stood before each of the amazon saints. One after the other looked back at me with eyes of Lwanga. I blessed myself with my red beads and sat down in my reading chair.

Ten meters away, before the eucalyptus copse, a Nandi Flame was catching the morning sun with its red orange flowers and tossing it to me through the window. I thought of Christ on the cross.

Lwanga is not a Christ, I thought. For sure, Lwanga is not a Christ; he is a male-Mary, a red male- Mary. His eyes are in the eye sockets of the male-Marys on the wall.

His are the eyes of Liberte climbing the barricade, who holds in one hand the tricolor flag (liberty, equality, fraternity) and who with her free hand signals me to climb with her over the top.

For several minutes I stare at Liberte and imagine myself with her, over the barricade, needle in hand, slaying diphtheria, tuberculosis, and other enemies of the people. I see the Bastille

---

[30] *Anaawarita* – A saint and martyr of the Congo.

[31] *Bhakita* – A freed slave of the Sudan, also a saint.

[32] *Donna Beatrice* – A queen of the Congo who evangelized her country centuries before the 19th century missionary movement.

[33] *Uwezo wa uzazi* – The power of maternal zeal.

fall, and whisper to the holy amazon still holding the tricolor, "Lwanga, my captain, I love you."

That afternoon I push the wheelbarrow with three large boxes of books through the store door. I unload the books in the chat corner.

Lwanga sees me, but cannot come. He is at the counter talking with Naibis, the book supplier.

Once I've taken the books out of the boxes, there are several piles of books surrounding the drumtable. They circle the drum like trees around a water hole.

In the meantime Lwanga has finished with Naibis and has gone in to his apartment. He comes out carrying a tray of *mandazis* and a pot of Mount Kenya. Making his way through the book forest, Lwanga knocks over Cervantes. After placing the tray on the drumtable, he goes back and remounts the Spanish knight. Turning again to the drumtable, Lwanga pours the coffee and says, "What is all this?"

"Our comrades home to roost," I said.

"These don't roost," said Lwanga. "They fly."

The coffee was hot and rich. He must have opened a new bag today, I thought. The *mandazis* were also fresh and crisp. I hate soggy *mandazis*.

Leaning back in the chair, I rested my elbow on a stack of books at the top of which lay the Ramayana. "Do you remember," I asked Lwanga, "the story you told me about Pseudo Buddha?" The storekeeper nodded. "Well," I said, "if the choices are flight or fight; I'll fight."

Lwanga put down his cup. "I've surmised that," he said. He was gazing at me with affection. His face reminded me of the mothers in the maternity ward, how the mothers look when they are first given the newborn baby to hold.

"To be precise," I said, "I'm going to work for the City Health Department. I'll be a member of an immunization team working in Eastlands. The campaign begins next week."

"Good, Rama." Lwanga beat the drumtable. "That's very good, Rama." He stood up, looked out the window, pointed east and said, "Victory to the infants in Eastlands." Turning to me he said, "The zeal of R. G. be with you."

After Lwanga had pointed out the window and just as he was turning back to me, at that instant, I saw in my mind's eye the painting of Delacroix appear, it occupied the entire space of the chat corner.

I was in a daze. Ibisaji helped me out of it by laughing at his own theatrics. He played the William Tell Overture on the drumtable and said, "Do what you can Rama, but don't take yourself too seriously."

I record Lwanga's last comment to give an accurate account of my coming-out-as-a-red, but I wonder why he said it. A fighter has got to take himself seriously.

Lwanga began to return the cups, saucers, and spoons to the serving tray. "Put all these books back in the boxes and the boxes back into the wheelbarrow and carry everything back to Lower Hill. Naibis the book supplier just told me that she'll restock the store with the same titles. She said that you'll need to reread these books. She thinks that now you're a graduate you'll need lectio now more than ever."

Martys' Blood, 1978, 1979

Rama, Wasomaji, August 25, 1979

I worked with the Eastlands immunization campaign for two years and I liked it. Fighting against corrupt colleagues, however, I didn't like. So when a transfer came I was not disappointed. The city made me assistant manager of the municipal blood bank. I drew blood from donors and kept records. In the second month I noticed an irregularity. The amount of blood I drew was more than the amount of blood sent to KNH. When this discrepancy appeared again, in the third month, I went to the bank manager.

"You're telling me that you collect more blood than we send to KNH," said the bank manager.

I was sitting on a low wooden stool facing my boss who sat on a high, upholstered chair behind a large desk. "Yes, sir," I said.

"Oh sorry," said the bank manager. "No one told you that some of the blood goes to Pumwani Maternity. It does not show up on the KNH records."

With hands under my thighs I sat up on the stool. "Then, sir, I'd like to be seeing all dispatch orders. That would tighten our internal control."

The bank manager stood up and said, "Thank you, doctor for making that suggestion. I will certainly look into it. Good day."

Nothing happened. Half a year went by and every month I noticed that a quarter of the donated blood disappeared unrecorded. Finally I went to Pumwani Maternity and asked the nurses there how much blood they were receiving from us each month. They told me that Pumwani had never received blood from the municipal blood bank.

I returned to the bank manager. "Sir, I must report the situation..."

He cut me short and glowered. "What do you want, Doctor? A cut?"

I was stunned. I couldn't say anything at the moment, but the next day I stormed into the bank manager's office and shouted, "I'm reporting you to the police, Sir."

The bank manager smiled an evil smile. "Don't be stupid, Doctor. I can give you five percent of the take."

I stood up and slammed my fist on the desk. "Sir, I just told you that I'm blowing the whistle on you. The scam is over. And you are over. Our city cannot tolerate the corrupt likes of you."

"Get out!" shouted the bank manager. Then he stood up, facing me, and, with both hands, gripped the edge of his desk. "Leave my office this instant!"

Ignoring him I continued, "To sell the blood sacrificed by people of good will, who donate it for innocent children.... is demonic. I cannot think of anything worse. You, sir, stink."

Nothing happened when I reported the blood bank manager to the police. Twice I filed a detailed and substantiated charge of corruption. No results. In the end I quit my job at the municipal blood bank.

A notion came to my head. I went to Readers' Guide to talk it over with Lwanga. We were sitting in the chat corner. It was late afternoon, a few minutes before closing time. The store was empty.

"I'll start my own blood bank," I said. "A Catholic one. I'll name it 'Martyrs' after Charles Lwanga and his companion Readers slain with him."

Lwanga was fingering his beads as he listened to me. My elaboration of the project took about half an hour. When I finished, Lwanga asked me where I would get the finances. That was not yet clear, I told him. "I'll give you my savings," he said. "What I've saved for new books I'll give you. Books, blood, what's the difference?"

The first year was a struggle. The most difficult task was recruiting blood donors. Martyrs had to gain the public's confidence. I tried two tactics. First, I submitted my documentation on the municipal blood bank to the newspapers. This knocked the competition off the field. Second, I recruited new donors with a high pressure campaign using the slogan, "Blood: Your Surplus Belongs to the Child."

Admittedly that initial campaign was meant to trigger guilt in potential recruits. The word, "Child", however was essential to the slogan because Martyrs Blood bank was devoted exclusively to the blood needs of children.

The campaign absorbed me. I went to colleagues, friends, and family to ask for blood. I drew blood from thousands of Nairobians and by the third year Martyrs Blood bank had a large enough reservoir to supply a thousand surgery cases annually.

Lwanga came one day to see me at Martyrs' Blood. "You've come back too soon," I said. Lwanga had just donated blood a few days earlier.

"I haven't come to donate blood today," he said. "I want to share a concern I have about you and lectio."

"Oh?"

"May I sit down?"

"Please."

Lwanga was wearing leather sandals. He had two earrings now. On his head he wore a red bandana, but I could still see the dreadlocks that dangled on his long neck and forehead. When he sat down, his back remained perfectly straight. He had the posture of a fashion model. His head was ever straight on his neck as if he were carrying a stack of invisible books. I saw him once carry water on his head like a woman. He did it for me the day he told me how R. G. Marie and the women followers of Jesus had carried earthen jars of water to Calvary to slacken the thirst of the crucified. Jesus never tasted it, but every drop of water intended for him turned to wine.

Sitting there that day in my busy office, Lwanga told me not to forget lectio. It isn't necessary to quote him here in detail. He was just worried that I was too busy to read...

Fellow Redbeads, listen. Lwanga is right. Let's not forget lectio! Readers must do lectio. In my spare time I try to do what I can.

Of course a committed Redbead has very little spare time, but no matter. Look at the accomplishment: on the fifth anniversary of Martyrs Blood bank we count five thousand children served with lifesaving transfusions! Much has been accomplished. Do you wonder how?

Quite simple. At Martyrs we stood against corruption. We stood against despair. And the city stood with us. A Red day dawns for "The City of the Sun![34]"

---

[34] Editor's note: The tourist agencies refer to Nairobi as the "Green City in the Sun." Rama has changed Green to Red to suit his own reading of Nairobi.

Part Two

An Introduction to Part Two: Portraits

Liberita

You have seen in our story thus far that Agio, Rama, and Lwanga like to make pictures. Even though Agio is the only one who is a professional painter, all three love to create images. Making pictures, especially out of words, is a faculty unique to *Homo Sapiens*. As with all faculties, this one weakens when not exercised, which unfortunately often happens in a television culture. TV culture is awash in images, but they are mass-produced and already processed. The viewer exercises the faculty of image-making or imagination very little because the images have little mystery, the images are obvious and finished in every detail; they leave little to the imagination. Books have more mystery; word pictures do not exist until the moment a Reader creates them with the mind's eye. Books invite the imagination to make its own pictures. What follows are pictures, or portraits, important to the Nairobi Circle of Readers.

Some people may be tempted to skip over descriptive writing because reading it is too much work, and I certainly have done the same countless times. You and I cheat ourselves of an imaginative experience, however, when we do this because to read is to make pictures in the mind. Part Two, Portraits, is a gymnasium where your image-making faculty will be exercised. The other three Parts are imagination gymnasiums, too. They will also give your imagination a good stretch. By the end of this book you should have a more muscular imagination because of all the exercise we've provided. The best way to benefit from the six portraits that follow is to sit quietly in front of each one and look at the portrait in a non-aggressive, almost passive way, and then your imagination muscle will just start working on its own. Then, indeed, perceptions and insights – the rewards of lectio – will follow.

The first of the six portraits is the only one I wrote. I wanted the Reader to first have an image of Naibis, the portrait-maker, in his mind while reading the five portraits she wrote. Naibis' first portrait of Agio was written in 1979 when he was in his prime (color). Naibis's first portrait of Rama was also written in 1979 when he too was in his prime (color). Naibis' second portrait of Agio was written in 1994 when he was at midlife, when he was at the end of his first adulthood, when his prime was fading. Naibis' second portrait of Rama was written in 1998 when not only his prime was faded, but even coats of red he added on red were peeling off. These four portraits are Naibis's personal reflections from her journal, and have never before been published.

Naibis also wrote a portrait of the Readers' Guide Bookstore. She wrote this fictional visit to the empty bookstore in May 2000. It appeared as a periodic advertisement in the *Wasomaji* from June 2000 up until September 2001. What was Naibis' purpose in portraying a visit and a chat at the old bookstore? It was simply this. She thought it would spark interest. She was hoping to give tours there so that Greenbeads and Redbeads could discover in that hallowed place their shared heritage. Naibis believed that remembering Readers' Guide would restore the experience of lectio. She always included these lines of Emily Dickinson in the tour ads:

> And this bequest of wings
> Was but a book.
> What liberty
> A loosened spirit brings.

Whenever I read those lines in the *Wasomaji* tour ads I thought of Naibis – she is, for me, and for many others here, the reading spirit of Nairobi. Just look at her name. "Naibis" combines the name of our city plus the name of the bird that represented the god of reading in ancient Africa. Even cities outside Africa might consider the phrase. Perhaps the reading spirit of Paris could be called Paribis, the reading spirit of Lima Limibis, that of Delhi Delhibis, that of Sydney Sydnibis, that of Boise Boisibis. Every place has a reading spirit that makes it readable. A final note to the Reader of these portraits. Agio and Rama, after the death of Lwanga, are haunted people. The bookstore, after the death of Lwanga, is a haunted place. As you're reading about these haunted people and this haunted place, remember that it is not a presence that haunts them, but an absence. What's most frightening is what's missing.

The Portrait of Naibis:
The Writer and Book Supplier

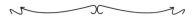

Liberita

I met Naibis four years ago. Today, as I sit in the Wasomaji office, I want to describe the physical appearance of this unusual lady.

Naibis is right now standing by the city desk, talking to a reporter. She is wearing an olive green dress that reaches down to mid-calf. Though old, the dress is newly seamed. It is belt less, and hangs on her high shoulders like drapery. Naibis always wears loose-fitting clothes, but she does not appear sloppy or careless in her habiliment. Her clothes are simple, clean, and neat.

Naibis decorates herself with many beads. She has a Maasai bracelet on her right hand, it is made of red and blue and yellow beads. She has a beaded necklace on today with green and brown beads, these are little and wooden and lie on her chest by the weight of a small cross at the end. Oh, I'm mistaken. Looking more closely I see she is wearing a rosary around her neck. Many Catholics in Nairobi do this. There is nothing over-pious in it. And the rosary Naibis is wearing is small enough that it fits like a necklace and seems quite right on her.

So much for her attire; now to the body.

Why is it that people who spend their days around books have the appearance of birds? Librarians look like birds. And so do many who work in bookstores. The easiest way to start describing the body form of Naibis is to write the word, "birdish."

As I watch Naibis with the reporter, I see her bony shoulders and how they rise from the middle of her back and extend out in a fan, like wings, above her clavicle. Yes, her shoulders are bony, and her long fingers too, and her long legs too. In limb, Naibis is bony and long but not heavy; her skeletal frame, one imagines, could bear feathers as easily as skin and hair.

Naibis' most striking physical trait is her neck and head. I mean the way her head is put on her neck. It seems that her long neck is made differently than a human neck. It must have sinews in unusual places that enable her to move her head a full 200 degrees both to the right and to the left. Birds have necks that let them swivel their heads like this. Birds, I think, need this because their eyes don't swivel enough.

Oh yes, the eyes.

Naibis has large eyes. In this she is unlike a bird. They have small eyes. The eyes of this odd-bird supplier are oceans. Hers take everything in and everything is let to sink down, deep down into those watery eyes. I should mention here that Naibis needs spectacles to see things at a distance. But she doesn't need them for reading. She keeps the spectacles on a string around her neck, and they dangle a bit lower than the rosary beads. Her frames are not round. Naibis prefers the type with upper tips that look like wings.

I see that today Naibis is wearing house slippers. She often does. Big, cushioned house slippers on her big, big feet. Really, her feet are so big! She even jokes about that.

As for hairstyle, Naibis cuts her hair close. She has just enough hair to hold a pencil, which I can see on the left side of her head. Oh my, how she gets annoyed when she has to go hunting for a pencil!

For Naibis, a writing instrument is as much a part of the human body as a beak is part of the body of a bird. Naibis is proud of her name, which combines Nairobi and Ibis.

Why the Egyptians associated the God of Letters with the ibis I don't know. An ibis does only one thing that resembles writing. When it pecks at the ground for food, its lengthy, thin beak looks like a stylus (which might make someone imagine the earth to be a scroll of papyrus). Otherwise the ibis does not behave like a writer. For one thing, it is too gregarious. Ibises like to be with other ibises. They don't make big assemblies like gulls but they always move in pairs, sometimes in threes and fours. A retiring, antisocial bird I think would have more in common with a writer.

Another way the ibis is different than the writer is its preference for the ground. An ibis spends a lot of time on the ground hunting grubs in the dirt. It sometimes takes wing and likes to make circles; but the ibis never soars. Wouldn't the inspirational writer be more like a falcon, the highest-flying bird? The falcon sees all. The falcon moves in the big picture. Its world is not at the end of its beak. It is not obsessed like the ibis. The falcon has other interests and a larger view of reality than the ibis who is fixed on a postage-stamp-sized, grub-infested patch of muddy soil. The pragmatic ibis reminds me more of a nurse who changes bedpans than a novelist whose inner screen is large enough for panorama.

One day I will ask Naibis why the Egyptians associated ibis with the God of Letters when the bird is so different from the writer. I may learn something about the ibis, or perhaps unlearn something about writers.

Portrait of Agio and Rama

A Portrait of Agio at 32

Naibis, 1979

"The Child," (a nickname which Agio encourages) is not
child-sized. That's why he doesn't enjoy climbing the seven
flights of stairs to the *Wasomaji* office. "The Jolly Green Giant" (a
nickname Agio discourages) posts most of his essays to the
Wasomaji; he is not often seen in Victoria House. Nonetheless, I
do have one illuminating encounter to record.

Agio and I are sitting together on a park bench in Jevanjee
Garden (the little park in front of Victoria House). It is middle
December. The short rains are over and the trees beginning to
green. Agio is watching a mama weaverbird whose diligent nest
making is being frustrated by an overbearing spouse who prefers
the lower branches. Agio makes a point about it (which I didn't
get) that makes him chuckle.

He hands me a large manila envelope. Inside is a picture of a
composite animal: part wildebeest, part warthog, a fabulous beast.
He asks me to print it in the Wasomaji for April first and say that
it was sighted in the Nairobi National Park. *The Nation*[1] always
does an April Fool picture. Why not the *Wasomaji*? He giggled a
kid's giggle, "Hee, hee, hee," and then a Santa Claus belly laugh,
"Ho, ho, ho." With his body still shaking that proverbial bowl full

---

[1] *The Nation* - Kenya's largest daily newspaper.

of jelly, he looked at me with eyebrows raised, and said, "We Christians sometimes take ourselves too seriously, don't you think?"

Let me freeze that scene and describe the joker sitting next to me on the park bench.

Agio is lighter skinned than Rama. He has the soft brown complexion one would expect when Italy marries Kenya. And that curly hair you see resting on his wide shoulders is also lighter (and softer) than the curls of Rama.

"Soft" is a word that exercises itself quite a bit in any description of Agio. His eyes are soft (and green), his mouth is soft, his musculature is soft, his hands and feet are soft. He is soft and gentle like a dairy cow in the lush fields of middle December.

Agio is careful about his clothes. He is "smart" as we say in Nairobi. Today he is wearing a laundered pink shirt and a green v-neck sweater. He has on a pair of tailored trousers from Armand's. His black leather shoes are imported, and they were probably polished this morning. In habiliment Agio is ever the artist. The style of the clothes fit the size of the man and the colors relate kindly to each other.

Now, I observe Agio in motion once again. He is still laughing. He wipes a tear from his rosy cheek with a fresh handkerchief. He grins at me, and his eyes are still glimmering with moist joy and mischief. "Thanks," he says, patting the manila envelope on my lap. He then makes a loopy gesture, what dramatists call a flourish. Agio loves to gesture in slow, soothing arches, never pointing a finger or clenching a fist. "Good-bye, my dear."

Agio stands up and holds my hand, "Be well," he says with a sincere though floppy handshake.

Off he goes. Despite the man's girth he doesn't wobble. He knows how to shift his weight to perambulate with grace. Agio doesn't walk quickly though. He's never in a hurry. I see him stroll down the park lane holding his hands behind his back looking at the trees about him. As he exits the park I hear him begin to whistle a Christmas carol.

A Portrait of Rama at 29

Naibis, 1979

My encounters with the doctor take place in Victoria House, which stands on the University side of Jevanjee Gardens. The *Wasomaji* office is located on the seventh floor of Victoria House. The old building has no lift so one really has to want to see me to see me.

Rama always runs up the seven floors. He takes two stairs at a time. When he reaches my office he is usually panting, but won't sit down to catch his breath. He prefers to stand in front of the window that frames the city skyline and raise the typed pages of his essay toward Nairobi, declaring, "This will change that."

This man who is shaking his fist at the window in my office is half Luo, half Indian. He has dark brown skin and loose curly hair. The skin is the beautiful color you'd expect from the mix of melanin that his parents gave him. The swirl in his curls was also what you'd expect at the confluence of the Nile and the Ganges. Rama's eyes! Here the Nilotic is absent. The doctor's eyes are fierce like the eyes of an enraged bull. They resemble the battlefield eyes of Indra just before he lets fly a spear of lightning at the evil Ashuras. The other curious thing about Rama's eyes (as he stands in the window frame of the *Wasomaji* office) is that he doesn't blink. His eyes never close. It is a bit scary. What of Rama's physique? Well, he is not imposing. He is short and thin. He can't weigh more than forty kilos. If he ever fell out that window, the wind would carry him a while before he hit the ground.

Rama's apparel? He's not well dressed. He is disheveled to put it politely; to tell the truth, he is a sloppy mess. His trousers are too big and hang too low on his waist (he probably doesn't even unzip them to take them off). I see the trousers are also stained with coffee and cigarette ash. And his plastic shoes? They haven't been polished since he bought them at Bata's four years ago. His trademark red sweater that he wears even at noon in the hot season? It is torn in five places and it's a size too small for him; he bought the thing in standard eight. His white shirt is frayed at the collar and dark with sweat. Rama smells okay so he must shower every day but his clothes probably get a wash every couple weeks, if that.

Ah, but Rama in animation? As he is talking to me, he rushes forward at me like a Marine with a bayonet. Rama never strolls, or walks. He always pushes ahead, advances, as if the air has to be penetrated. His gait is fast and he keeps his head slightly down like a rhino does when running. The verb I think which best describes Rama in animation is: "Charge!" When I watch him in motion I can almost hear the William Tell Overture.

I don't want to be harsh with the man. But there he is. And that is how he looks. Rama is fixed on one thing. He is burning up with it, and he is oblivious to clothing and demeanor. He makes me think of someone who has just been knocked down by a big bully and is about to pounce on the monster like a leopard would pounce on a water buffalo. Rama is a scrapper, and he never gives up on a fight. He'll hit back even when he's pinned. If he were completely unable to move his limbs, crucified to the ground, he would spit, bare his teeth, and growl.

Portrait of Agio at 47

Naibis, 1994

The death of Lwanga marked the beginning of Agio's acedia. The loss has dried him up. Slowly, as if he were bleeding from his pinky for two years. That is what I have witnessed from 1992 until 1994 when I visited him in his studio.

Even Agio's studio has suffered acedia. I found the palettes caked with dry paint. The dusty shelves held bottles of solidified green, blue, and yellow. The air too was stale and vaporless as February.

The acedia is most evident in Agio's face. A fat jolly man, he has become prunish and narrow-eyed. His skin has lost its shine, and it too is caked and flaked like the paint on his unfinished canvases. When I knock, he unlatches the door and lets me in without even a hello. He relatches the door with jerky hands. Everything about him is spasmodic. His body-actions are often nothing more than nervous reflexes. His limbs move about without a purpose or a purpose forgotten – he will want to itch himself on the arm, for example, and then forget why his hand was near the arm and grab it instead, holding himself.

After relatching the door he lets me follow him to a sofa in the studio. He agitates slowly on brittle bones. Sitting close by him and him not saying a word was a new experience – his flowing mouth is a dry gulley. All he did is sigh. "Idleness" is often used as a synonym for acedia. But the sinfulness in acedia is not as machine-age-men imagine when they condemn laziness, and other offenses against the work ethic. The sinfulness in acedia, according to Thomas Aquinas, is that one no longer consents to be a full self, one is overcome with sadness (*tristitia saeculi*) when faced with the goodness in oneself – because the will to realize that good has disappeared.

According to Aquinas, acedia is a sin against the third commandment, a violation of Sabbath rest. One does not consent to be, to enjoy being; one despairs of existence. Acedia, then, is the opposite of leisure.

Agio is indeed suffering acedia. Though he cannot paint, neither can he sit as before and do creative nothing. After so many sighs on the sofa he gets up, goes to the window, comes back to the sofa, and then a minute later gets up again, goes to the shelves with the solidified colors to hold the bottles or rearrange the bottles. He no longer keeps beads in his hands, instead he fingers a rubber band that he stretches between his thumb and forefinger, releases, stretches again and releases. He gets up to go to the toilet three or four times in the hour I spend with him. He never sits down for more than five minutes. Restless, always restless; yet afraid of rest.

Portrait of Rama at 48

Naibis, 1998

Lwanga's death was the beginning of Rama's indolence. When the Keeper of Thoth died so did Rama's desire to read. He went cold. Since 1992, Rama has pretended he was hot, the passionate red doctor. But the zeal is out. He is a tired man. He still calls himself an "activist" but he has no faith in the consequences of action. Nothing is going to get better in Nairobi. When Rama stopped bringing articles, I decided to go to him. As a fellow Reader, I wanted to be with him during his bereavement.

Rama is usually asleep when I arrive. Even when I've roused him from bed and he is sitting behind his desk, his eyes remain cloudy and sometimes his head will nod and he'll fall back asleep in mid-sentence. The man is spent. Even his clinic is exhausted. Diplomas and citations are not straight on the wall, they droop on the string. The dustbin is overflowing with wads of paper. There is garbage everywhere. The coffee stained rug is covered with crumbs of scones. The coffee table has six plates of unfinished meals (though fruit flies are doing their best to finish the rotten bananas). Rama's desk is covered with broken pencils and pages ripped out of books, as well as the debris of his profession – broken needles, balls of bloody cotton, cracked thermometers, old bandages, and used transfusion tubing.

Let me add something more about Rama's appearance. Each time I go to see him, the state of his disrepair is worse. His lab coat is more torn and filthy, though he wore it as faithfully as a nun does her habit. His hair is more matted and wild from more pillow time. His whiskers are longer, grayer, and more unkempt.

His hands are the most remarkable aspect of his changing appearance. His fingernails have grown longer and longer. The dirt in them has increased too. He bothers less with cleaning his hands because he uses them less – less for vaccine campaigns, less for fingering beads. Even when we talk together he gestures less and less. It was as though Rama's hands have lessened to nothing but a piece of waste tossed atop the heap of trash in the clinic of Martyr's Blood. Now he doesn't use his hands at all, he just holds them in his lap. He holds them in contempt.

You may wonder what Rama and I talk about. Well, here too, the mess factor is evident. In rambling. In non sequitor. His sentences don't connect. He lets words spill from his mouth like loose stool. His speech has bits and pieces of undigested information and nothing held together. Like CNN, only worse. Whenever I listen to him and look at him three nouns echo in my mind: Indolence, Ennui, Waste. These add up to one word, despair. Not just any despair; Raman despair. While a leisurist might despair in being, a legionnaire despairs in doing.

He didn't have to say it (and he wouldn't), but everything I saw of him and his habitat illustrated apostasy. He didn't burn with *uzazi* zeal. It was out like cold ash.

Recently, on my way out of the blood bank, I noticed the icon of the Perpetual Helper behind the donor registration desk had been altered. The hand of R. G. Marie (which holds the shoe of the Child) was cut to pieces. That part of the canvas was a heap of scrap. Later that week I received a large envelope on which was typed Rama's return address. Inside it I found an old piece of transfusion tubing and a "Rama in Ruin" note:

> Nothing works. Nothing will get better.
> Earth follows not the law of love,
> it follows the law of entropy.
> Everything tends toward dissolution
> and waste.
>
> *Rama in Ruin*

We Come of Age as Masks

No one lives his life,
Disguised since childhood,
Haphazardly assembled
From voices and fears and little pleasures,

We come of age as masks.
Our true face never speaks.

Somewhere there must be storehouses
Where all these lives are laid away
Like suits of armor or old carriages
Or clothes hanging limply on the walls.

Maybe all paths lead there,
To the repository of unlived things.

Rilke

Portrait of a Haunted Bookstore

With You Among Empty Shelves

Naibis, Wasomaji, 2000, 2001

Here we are. This was a bookstore.

_____?

Readers' Guide. The store was called Readers' Guide. See the faded paint above the front window? Can you make out the colors? Each letter of Reader is alternately red and green. At one time a signboard above the sidewalk asked the passerby "Are you looking for Readers' Guide?"

_____?

I know you are. Come in, come in. *Karibu.* Let's sit down over there by the front window. Aren't you tired? I am. It's a long walk from the train station.

Hoooaa. Man, that feels good. I love these old chairs.

Take your shoes off, go ahead. Your socks, too. Make yourself comfortable. You've traveled a distance.

It's great to have you here. I've so much to tell you. If you can stay in Nairobi two nights we'll have this afternoon and two full days. Is that possible?

_____.

Wonderful! I know you are hungry. The coffee is brewing and the scones are baking. Would you like to eat first or may I start now?

_____.

Good. Where shall I begin?

_____.

Oh yes, let me begin with the bookstore. Readers' Guide is the object of your visit.

_____?

This spot where we're sitting? It's the chat corner. Here the previous storeowner used to discuss books with his customers. The window faces west so in the afternoon the sun lit the place with its strength and beauty, like now. A fuchia plant was suspended just behind my head. And its little upside down pink white flowers were ballerinas dancing spotlighted in the sun. Between our chairs was a drumtable. The previous owner thought every bookstore should have one. Ancestors live in drums and books, he said. And Readers' Guide had the largest collection of books in Nairobi.

Look at the four walls and the built-in shelves. They go eleven feet up. The green books were there.

In the middle of the room – see where the floorboard is warped? – stood shelves eight feet high. The red books were there.

A bookstore has many pleasures, Readers' Guide especially. I spent hours with its books, browsing among the red in the middle and the green at the sides. The previous storeowner understood this. He even added to his customers' enjoyment. Every morning and afternoon he would serve them buttered scones and fresh coffee. "Relax, stay a while," he used to tell them.

Readers' Guide was homey because the owner lived here.

_____?

See where I'm pointing, that door at the far end? It opens into a little apartment where the owner had a bed, stove, and a kitchen table. Also there is a screened porch attached to the kitchen where he used to read.

_____?

Store atmosphere? I would say bright and airy. The windows of Readers' Guide were usually open.

_____?

Colors? The ceiling and walls were painted gold. The pillars at the four corners of this room were painted in stripes of red and green, like candy canes.

The previous owner liked carpets. He had three Persian carpets on this floor. One had animals from popular African fables, another had Bible scenes, and in the third an ibis was woven.

_____?

The basement below is where Lwanga would give reading lessons to children he was sponsoring in school. In his literacy classes students learned to read a text in the context of their social and political situation.

_____?

The story above is a classroom. It once had about thirty cushions scattered on the floor with a red and green striped chair in the middle where the storeowner would sit and recite poetry; most often Swahili Psalms. The assembly would then do lectio on the text.

_____?

I'll explain lectio later.

_____?

Way up at the very top? It's a loft. A ladder in the poem room reaches the loft but was seldom used. Only Lwanga visited the loft, because only he dared. The loft is where the holy Ibis lived. Lwanga fed the Ibis three times a day. Sometimes, according to hearsay, Lwanga went up to the loft to talk to the Ibis. Certain customers even claimed that Lwanga controlled the Ibis and could make the Ibis go places and do things. They said that Lwanga was the master of the Ibis. However, when asked about the bird, Lwanga would reply, "I am not the Master of Thoth, I am the Keeper of Thoth." The Ibis, as Lwanga would always remind people, was the symbol of the African God of Reading, Thoth.

I must admit I wondered about Lwanga spending so much time in the loft. But I did not wonder about the places the Ibis visited when it jumped of the loft window ledge, took flight, and didn't come back for hours. Do you have any questions?

_____?

In English, perhaps the keeper of an ibis would be called an Ibiser as the keeper of falcons is called a falconer, but Swahili speakers don't like the sound of "-er" much. So, Lwanga was called Ibisaji.

_____?

Readers' Guide. Lwanga chose that name in 1963 when he opened the store. He named it after R. G. Marie. As you know her first two initials stand for Readers' Guide. The early Christians called her that because she was the first human being to read the Word. She conceived it, gave it birth and later taught the Word to read words. Lwanga was so excited by the mystery that he wanted to found a monastic order that would develop a Marian yoga of reading.

It never came to be. Lwanga's movement split into two factions, Redbeads and Greenbeads. The Ibisaji had to give up his idea of a monastery. No loss, I'd say. If it were an order, Readers would have been strictly controlled by the Magesterium. But as a lay movement there are fewer restrictions. Members can even marry if they want. Though many, like Lwanga, Rama, and Agio never did.

_____?

Lwanga himself? One could describe him in two ways – the red way and the green way. Let me describe Lwanga first in the red way; I will tell you about a portrait. Actually it was hanging right there on the west wall of the bookstore. A painting of Lwanga that Rama created. Let me restore it for you.

The painting is four feet high and two feet wide. Lwanga is standing, a long slender man, twenty-six years old, a furrowed brow on the young face. Anger? Worry? A square chin with day old black fuzz. The ebony face is long and the bones in it are prominent. Especially the bone around the eyes. The eyes are set deep in the bone, burning like two bonfires. The black hair is in dreadlocks and touches the collar of a leather jacket that appears to be too small. There is a pen behind the left ear, and a toothpick between lips that seem too soft for toothpicks. The body itself is muscular but not showy. The muscles are not for adornment, they are for carrying loads. The upper body presses against an unseen gale. The lower body is all push, the legs are powerful like those of a soccer player. But this man does not play games. His look is earnest. In it is something of death stared down. He turns his head around to look at you, his chin is over the right shoulder as he calls to you, the rest of his skeleton pressing forward. He's a step ahead of you. He is walking fast. And he is pointing at something ahead of him that he wants you to see.

There you have him, Lwanga the Ibisaji. Or should I say you have him as Rama had him. Now let me describe Lwanga in the green way; again I will tell you about a portrait. Let's imagine it together.

Agio's Lwanga is a tall, slender, young man with a broad welcoming smile. He's got long fingers with an emerald ring on the left index, and long feet in green sandals. Picture it for yourself. And note the eyes. Set deep in his chocolate face, those large round eyes twinkle with a green light. I can't tell if the iris is green or if the eye merely reflects a green vision.

_____?

You want to go look at the painting up close? Go ahead! Let's imagine together.

_____!

Green, so you agree with me! But "warm," too, you say. You're very observant. Agio used to say Lwanga's eyes were warm as a bread oven and mellow as a late night campfire. Agio told me that in Lwanga's gaze he could stretch out and let the comfort unhinge sinews and muscles as happens to a tired body close by a late night campfire. And after an hour in this relaxing heat Agio said he could hardly stand up. And his body, he said, took pleasure in the deep earth pull of gravity. A paradox – getting high on gravity!

_____.

Yes. He does look like a Swahili sailor with his silver earring and his white cotton trousers waist-bound with a rope, and his unbuttoned blue jersey exposing a smooth muscled chest and thin gold chain. Every inch a sailor. Agio used to say that Lwanga moved his body like a dhow fisherman. Dhow (Tao)[2] movements – jumping fore or aft or up the mast – are quickened. They come from the body, not from the head. Agio used to call this quickness of the body "graciness," but the quickness of the head, craziness. He said that a ballet dancer is gracy, but that Redbeads are crazy.

_____.

I know. You're here to read. Good. The readings are in the folders you just set on the drumtable. I'll be in the kitchen a while, and then I will bring you hot scones and fresh coffee. Read slowly. There's no rush. We have two days. As the Greenbeads are always telling the Redbeads, "You've got watches, we've got time."

Take your time then with these two folders. One contains the Confession of Rama. The other contains the Confession of Agio. These two pieces appeared earlier this year in serial form in the *Wasomaji*.

As you know, both Redbeads and Greenbeads are boycotting our newspaper to protest the publications you are now holding in your hand. The *Wasomaji* will soon be extinct because this boycott has made it impossible for us to keep the paper going. That is why I appreciate you, brave visitor. I am grateful that in an individual way you have broken the embargo by holding in your hands copies of the censored texts. Thank you for risking a visit to this haunted bookstore, for risking a discovery.

When you read the midlife confessions of a doctor and a painter you will understand more about yourself, even though you may not be a doctor, or a painter, or even middle-aged. The thing you will understand about yourself is why you are attracted to a haunted bookstore.

Let me tell you: every Reader has a Lwanga, a reading mentor. And each of us could give a portrait of our preferred guide with as much detail as Rama's painting of Red Lwanga or Agio's painting of Green Lwanga. What haunts each of us, though, is the phantom

---

[2] The *nature* of heaven and earth, its hidden way, and deep processes; its power to compensate; its balance and harmony; its grace.

guide and the store of books each of us has neglected up to this point in our lives.

You will read in these confessions the story of a haunted Redbead and a haunted Greenbead. Each of them is haunted by an absence in their lives. And that absence is as Rilke said, "a repository" of unlived days, of unlived desires, of the phantom self. If you don't believe me, do an experiment with red. Stare into solid red for a minute and then at blank white. Red's phantom will appear: green. Do the same experiment with green. Stare into solid green for a minute and its' phantom will appear: red. Now you see. Red is haunted by green; and green is haunted by red. In the presence of one you are haunted by the absence of the other. What the Leader of the Redbeads, and the Leader of the Greenbeads needed, in order to undo the haunting, as you'll see in these confessions, is to meet in each other the phantom guide they feared. And they had to do that here in this bookstore, which both leaders vigorously avoided since Lwanga's death.

I am glad that you, intrepid Reader, have come to the Readers' Guide. You are, unfortunately, one of the few to do so. It was my hope when I started these tours that by the end of the year 2000 I would have given at least a hundred Readers this tour. I thought that touring the bookstore and reading the confessions would restore the Circle of Readers. Now I would hazard to say that the faction leaders will need to do something more dramatic and public if this Circle is to be restored.

I haven't lost hope in a restoration. The day is not far off when this empty store will be filled with Redbeads and Greenbeads doing lectio together! And you, brave visitor, by coming here now have quickened the day. I appeal to anyone who still reads the *Wasomaji* and may have my article in hand to come here to this haunted bookstore. You, too, can quicken the day.

Ahh, that day! I can picture it in my mind's eye. This bookstore will be filled with a hundred Readers sitting in a circle. They will celebrate what is red and green: the Poinsettia, the Kenyan Flag, the Italian Flag, the Robes of Our Lady of Consolata, Blood and Chlorophyll, Chameleons.

The December Book will be in the hands of the Redbeads.
The March Book will be in the hands of the Greenbeads.

Ngugi Wa Thiongo will be sitting on Rama's lap.
Okot B. Bitek will be sitting on Agio's lap.

And arm in arm dancing with each other I see:
Edel Quinn and Karen Blixen
Quixote and Sancho
Camus and Wilde
Doctor Schweitzer and Doctor Suess
Nelson Mandela and Bill Cosby
Charles DeGaulle and Charlie Chaplin
Zoro and Zorba
Mark and Luke
Paulo Freire and Mathew Fox
Mother of Sorrows and Mother of Joys
Liberationists and Creationists

I see it in my mind. It will be like a wedding reception – two families celebrating their union with red and green bunting; with Reggae music and Viennese waltzes; and everyone will be eating Neapolitan ice cream. Oh for that blessed day, Oh for that wedding banquet, Oh for an end to this hostility.

I hope you quicken the day, dear Reader, by a visit to this empty bookstore. But if all you do is read my article then at least remember these words of a priest poet:

> Every creature is full of God and is a book about God. We are nature; we are volumes of revelation and books about God. [That which] urges us to create, to display, to tell our story is [of God]. Divinity is seeking to be revealed everywhere. "Every creature is doing its best to express God,"

says Meister Eckhart... We, because we are nature, and to the extent we live our authentic nature, are indeed one of the volumes of revelation. Like any book we need to be opened up, to be read, to be grasped, to be known.

Lectio of Mathew Fox on the writings of Meister Eckhart

Part Three

Introduction to Part Three

Liberita

The Confessions of a Doctor at Midlife and the Confessions of a Painter at Midlife[1] were not as widely circulated as the collection of writings that constituted Part One. The reason for this is that some of the Redbeads and Greenbeads who read the Confessions did not like the idea of the Circle of Readers being reunited. They started a boycott of the Wasomaji Newspaper to thwart the reunion these confessions advocated.

The motive of those who tried to have only the texts of Part One circulated is understandable. They wanted Hagiography, not Biography. But I say that Hagiography is a disservice to God's saints because it denatures holiness. The Reader is left with caricatures and robbed of characters.

And so, we've pulled out of our "confidential" file-drawer these two confessions. For real reconciliation truth is needed. Here you have it, naked truth. Rama confesses. Agio confesses.

Naibis and I feel we owe to our readers an explanation of the sequence of these two confessions. You will see that we have placed Rama's confession first even though Agio entered and came through his midlife transition before Rama. We've put Rama's midlife story first (though chronologically it comes second) for the sake of Kairos.

Nairobi Readers know that in the exercise of lectio, *Chronos* (clock-time) is less important than *Kairos* (opportunity-time). When one reads biographies one is always surprised that certain things cannot be explained by *Chronos*' science of cause and effect. With the biographies of Rama and Agio, there is a meta-order in the narration of their lives, which we as editors want to respect by sequencing the confessions of Rama and Agio in the

---

[1] The two confessions were printed in the same issue of the Wasamaji, the 22nd of Janurary 2000 edition.

way you have it. Naibis explains the way two middle-aged Readers evoke each other between the two confessions about Midlife Enantiodromia. It seemed to us that *Kairos* wanted the words of Naibis about evocation between the two confessions. *Kairos'* art of cause and effect is also honored by having Agio, in his confession, describing Lwanga's martyrdom just before the climax of *Two Readers* entitled "Readings at a Wedding of Opposites." We felt *Kairos* desired that order.

Finally, let me say something about my baby brother's death. Now I am not talking as an editor, but as a God-believer struggling to understand suffering. I will never accept that the death of a single child was necessary. And when I remember the day my baby brother died, I repeat a pledge I made then: Never Again! But I confess now to you that my personal motive for arranging this anthology of texts was to find a meaning to my baby brother's death. And, indeed, I did find it. For the more I worked on the manuscript the more I realized that the death of Taak[2] was the *Kairos* moment for the second half of life for Agio and Rama. I do not think that God who is the Editor of all lives made Taak die to convert two middle aged men, but I do believe that God used Taak's death for a redemptive purpose which you will soon read about. My hope is that when it happens to you, when your life becomes a difficult text, that you will be able to read meaning there; that you will be able to read more *Kairos* than chaos there.

---

[2] *Taak* – This word is the first word of a Maasai phrase meaning, "Be Your Full Self."

Confessions of a Doctor at Midlife

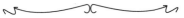

Redbeads, Come Back

Rama, January 22³, 2000

I appeal to Redbeads who refuse to pray the joyful mysteries to come back.

What are you doing?

Don't you know Nairobi?

This is a city of labor and leisure, red and green are the colors of our country's flag.

If you get stuck in the sorrowful mysteries you'll never attain glory.

Come back, Redbeads. Sit on the prayer carpet of many colored threads.

Be glorious.

Be catholic.

---

³ The feast of Fr. William Joseph Chaminade the founder of the Marianists. Chaminade saw Mary as Queen of Apostles, as the Leader and Teacher of communities in mission; *contemplative* communities in *active* mission. The Marianists started several Community Development Projects in Kenya during the eighties and nineties, these include: Maria House, Chaminade Training Center, Job Creation Program, Marianist Development Project and Our Lady of Nazareth Primary School. The Marianists were also responsible for Aquinas High School and Mangu High School, two of the finest secondary schools in Kenya.

Redbeads Come Back! (Preface to a Confession)

Rama, Wasomaji, January 22, 2000

Do I surprise you, Redbeads? You never thought you would hear me say: "Come Back to the Circle of Readers." But that is exactly what I am saying. Let us return and embrace the Greenbeads.

Are you bewildered, Redbeads? Are you asking yourselves, "What has happened to Rama? He is the leader of our faction, his red zealotry inspires it. What has gotten into him? Why has he changed?"

To answer these questions I have written a Confession. It was a confession of a personal nature, a confession spoken and written to an old friend, Agio. But, at the request of Liberita and Naibis, I have released the entire document to be published in the pages of the *Wasomaji*.

"Confessions of a Doctor at Midlife" will appear in serial form in the first few weeks of the new century. I urge Redbeads to read these issues of the *Wasomaji*.

If my confessions fail to reunite the Circle of Readers, I will try something else. What more can I do?

Should I go so far as to embrace Agio at the graveside of Lwanga?

I am willing.

Karura Forest, Night, January 1, 1999

Rama, Wasomaji, January 29, 2000

I snapped a photograph of it, of the blood dumping. I was standing on a tree stump in Karura Forest with my instamatic and pushed down on the red button.

Flash!

The strong white light showed what was happening in the dark forest. Two hundred sixty six gallons of blood were being poured into a round pit near some felled trees. My two attendants wanted to save the bags. I told them to throw them into the pool of blood.

I walked over to the van to get the jerry can of petrol. I had my hand on the lever of the sliding door but paused a moment to read the blistered words there. I remembered the day I painted them – the day I bought the van – that day twenty years ago when I launched Martyrs' Blood.

Slamming the door behind me with my left hand I carried the jerry can in my right. At the edge of the red pit I undid the top of the jerry can and poured in the petrol. Signaling my attendants to stand back I lit a match and threw it into the volatile mix. Whooosh – immense flames consumed the blood of four thousand two hundred and fifty four donors.

TV Room of Rama's Flat, Morning, January 2, 1999

Rama, Wasomaji, February 5, 2000

"Welcome to the KBC Earlybird News. I'm Patrick Njoroge.

"In October 1989, ten years after 1979, 'The Year of the Child,' our president and seventy others signed a promise to the world's children. This historic event took place during the World Summit for Children at the U. N. headquarters in New York.

"The doctors and nurses of Kenya have been working hard to fulfill these historic promises. According to Doctor Rama, who we interviewed earlier in the week, the two most important promises to come out of this Summit are to reduce the child mortality rate to 50 per 1000, and achieve universal immunization.

"Now, in October 1999, ten years after signing that promise, Kenya has not yet achieved what we promised. However, the campaign..."

I switched off the T.V. My face disappeared instantly but the screen flickered green-white for a few seconds before the glass became completely dark.

What could I do for distraction? I certainly didn't want to see myself on TV talking about reducing the child mortality rate. I was in no mood to hear about "The Campaign" after my day in Karura forest.

Feeling desperately bored, staring at the large selection of videocassettes on a shelf beside the TV, I heard something land on the verandah.

"Raaa Maaaa... Raaaa Maaaa... Raaaaa Maaaaa."

Without hesitation I grabbed the book at hand, *Medical Dictionary Volume One*, and stepped out onto the verandah.

"Raaa Maaaa... Raaaa Maaaa... Raaaaa Maaaaa." Lwanga's Ibis called to me mockingly.

"Oh, Ibis, Lwanga's Ibis! Why pursue me? Why haunt me? Leave me alone, Oh Reading Spirit. I'll not open a book again, and I'll not let you deceive another wide-eyed youth. I will destroy you before you misguide anyone else. Oh god -- awful bird, your wings of liberty will never open again. You dangerous bird, you hated thing; die, now!" I slammed the book down on the bird's head with the full force of both hands.

The Ibis fell to the stone pavement. It went down with a heavy thud, but something light, a wisp of air that sounded like a child's whistle, came from its lungs.

I kicked the fallen bird in the stomach. It didn't budge. It made no more noise. I knelt down and saw that its skull was cracked. A slow trickle of blood came out its beak.

I buried the Ibis under a thevetia tree in my backyard. When I came back into the house, the phone was ringing. I lifted the receiver with my left hand, still holding the shovel in my right.

"It's Agio. When can you give me an appointment, Rama?"

My hand tightened on the shovel handle. Agio? I had not seen him since 1994, purposely. I had no desire to see him, ever. I remained silent as his voice grew louder.

"Hello, Hello? Is this the residence of Doctor Rama? Tell him Agio wants an appointment."

Finally I spoke, proffering excuses. But he insisted... and insisted. So I gave in. I suggested the following morning. He accepted.

"Okay. Okay, tomorrow then," I said harshly and slammed down the receiver with an idea in mind to tell him off so he'd never bother me again.

Eating breakfast I kept wondering why he wanted to see me. What had he to complain about? I hadn't maligned him for 6 years. I had stopped writing for the *Wasomaji* the year Lwanga died.

Evening of the Same Day in TV Room of Rama's Flat

Rama, Wasomaji, February 12, 2000

I put on one of my old videos. I think it was "The Rise and Fall of Idi Amin." It was terrible. I turned off the VCR and stared at my shelf of two hundred-some cassettes. *What a waste of time,* I thought. Two hundred cassettes at an average of two hours apiece would come to four hundred hours. And none of it was any good. I got up from the divan removed the cassette and returned it to the shelf. To the right, perpendicular to the shelf, was another shelf of books. A sheet was draped in front of this bookcase, a white sheet I had not lifted since Lwanga's funeral. But that night, I thought, *Why not? It can't hurt...* I pulled back the sheet and read the title of the nearest book, *Leaves of Grass.* I reached for it, but then stopped myself. "Nonsense," I said out loud. "Waste, just more waste," I said still louder, as if talking to the book. I let the sheet fall.

That night I went to bed early. I slept for several hours and then woke up with a start. I sat up in the bed. "Who' s there?" I said. Silence answered. I looked about in the dark room wondering what had awakened me. Nothing seemed to have fallen. *Must have been dreaming,* I thought. But I did not lie back down. I pulled my knees up to my chin and stared down at the bed linen. My mind wandered...

...Lwanga's funeral, what an insult. My performance...

...His body is there in the ground, the dirt still heaped to the side of the hole. Men in ties are standing next to the heaps of red soil with shovel blades almost touching their black polished shoes. Their hands are folded on the shovel handles while they listen to the speeches.

I extol Lwanga in such a way that the shovelers think of me rather than him. I quote an American saying which was a favorite of his, "Pray for the dead and fight like hell for the living." Oh, they are surely thinking of me! Aren't I the one who fights like hell for the kids?

Then I launch into my attack. "Thus must we remember Lwanga. Better indeed to fight for the humanitarian ideals he stood for. Not by dedicating to him queer paintings having no social Message – so-called art whose message is only art." I continue on this theme for ten minutes.

Agio gives his burial oration next. He attacks me, and the Red I represent.

After our trade of eulogy insults the shovelers hold out to each of us a blade full of wet soil. Neither of us looks into the hole as we fling the mudballs down. We are glaring at each other...

The alarm clock sounded. *Good,* I thought. *Enough of that.* I got out of bed, showered, dressed, and ate breakfast. I was sitting securely behind my desk at 9 am when Agio arrived.

Rama's Office in Martyrs' Blood, Morning, January 3, 1999

Rama, Wasomaji, February 19, 2000

I did not stand when he entered the room. I pretended to be busy – the overworked doctor, behind the desk, head down, writing.

"Ahem," Agio cleared his throat. "Is this an inconvenient time?"

I kept up the show.

Agio sat down.

I swiveled the chair to face the bookshelves, pulled out something about measles and copied something from it.

Agio looked at me, and behind me, at the trophy table. He saw my license as a Blood Transfusionist, my Degree in Immunology, my award from UNICEF for immunizing fifty thousand children in twenty years, etc. Agio continued to take in the paraphernalia on the trophy table. I kept quiet. I didn't want to interrupt his inspection, hoping he'd believe I was still the champion of those trophies.

When I thought he was sufficiently impressed I put down my

pen and looked up, feigning surprise. "Oh, you've come. So get to the point. You can see I am very busy."

Agio smiled. It was a wonderful smile. He smiled in that warm way some people smile, with eyes lit up and cheek muscles natural. How to describe it? He was not smiling because he was nervous, or obliged. He was smiling at me, genuinely smiling at me, because of how he felt about me. And it would have been sunshine on my frozen face if I had let it touch me. "Are you hungry?" he asked.

"Hungry?"

"I've a picnic lunch. Come with me to the arboretum. We'll walk there, take in fresh air, enjoy ourselves. See that the day is bright and blue."

I slapped my hand on the desk and stood up, "That's what's wrong with you and all your kind. A picnic! Go for a picnic! Just like that. Don't you know, Agio, there's a war on. Do you realize that 4,000 children die every day from hunger and preventable diseases. Even an hour with you in the arboretum means not immunizing thirty children. What about that, Agio?"

To give my words more effect I put an arm akimbo and raised the other in front of me, pen in hand and pointing.

Oh, how grand!

See the swordsman defying those preventable diseases!

Agio was still smiling at me with that natural smile and said affably, "It's okay if you can't today, call me when you're free."

"Free!" I screamed. "I'm never free! A doctor is always on call. Especially a doctor like me. I must be ready at all times to rush blood to the victims of car crashes, land clashes, robberies, and other calamities. A body doesn't wait for blood. My phone rings from midmoming, after other doctors have finished rounds, through the whole day. Constantly, you hear? Riing Riiiing Riiiiiiing. 'Rama more blood, send us more blood.'"

I sat back down in my chair. I had made an impression. He had an image of me. Now I took the offensive. "And you, Agio. Look at your life, man. It is a waste. What have you done to make the world better? What suffering have you relieved? What suffering have you prevented? If we put the worth of your life in a balance it would weigh less than an ibis feather. Where are your deeds?"

And Agio smiled, a genuine affable smile.

I waited for rebuttal. He was good at rebuttal. We'd sparred for two decades in the *Wasomaji*.

But Agio said nothing to defend himself. He just looked at me and smiled some more.

"Get out," I said. "I've work to do."

He nodded, stood up, and reached out his hand to say good-bye. I didn't reciprocate. He looked at the ceiling and at his shoes. Finally, with a little sigh, he turned around, and quietly left the room. All the while I was writing something from the measles book.

That night I was awakened again. "Who's there," I said. No reply. I switched on the small lamp at the bedside. No power! I was suddenly afraid of the dark. My bed was next to the window so I pulled back the curtain. The moon was almost full and the small clouds flying by it were shining, one after another, lit in cold white. Then a bank of enormous clouds approached. I saw them roll over the Southern Cross and the Pleiades, and then the clouds completely covered the moon. The night was inky now. I let the curtain fall and lit a match. From the night table I picked up the photo of the blood dumping.

"Waste. Worthless waste," I said to the photo. "You are red and look useful but you won't do any good. There's no power in you. No immunity. You can't fight back. And worse – you'll take the power out of good blood."

The bedside lamp went on. I could hear the refrigerator start up. Electricity. I looked at the clock: 5:00 am.

I was still holding the photo. That annoyed me. How many times would I fish it out of my pocket or grab it off the night table? Why did I keep looking at it? I had to stop myself.

Another night lost. I threw back the blankets and got out of bed. I went to the bathroom to perform my morning rituals. It was while I was shaving that I noticed it. My eyes. I put down the razor, and. leaned over the sink for a better look. What's happened? Those are lizard eyes. Cold like a lizard's. Empty like a lizard's. Soulless like a lizard's. I was dead. I must be dead. Nobody's there behind those eyes.

Later in the Day in the Lab at Martyrs' Blood, January 4, 1999

Rama, Wasomaji, February 26, 2000

That afternoon an old classmate of mine came to the lab. After graduating from medical school, Dr. Z. had joined the Red Crescent and had served in several disaster areas: the Sahel in the mid-seventies, Mozambique in the early eighties, Ethiopia in the mid eighties, Somalia in the early nineties. In 1994 he was sent to Rwanda. He had just finished that assignment and was back home in Kenya waiting to begin work at a Red Crescent hospital in Turkana. Dr. Z. was a devout Moslem. He could recite many verses of the Koran. He knew the entire Sura on Mary by heart. In fact, he had a great love for Mary. He often prayed her mantra: "*uwezo wa uzazi.*"

Now, except for the Sahel, the disasters Dr. Z. had seen were manmade, war-made.

So I asked Dr. Z. about the battlefields. He described a few of the horrors he had lived through.

I asked him then what he thought of Homo Sapiens. As he saw neighbor killing neighbor didn't he think human beings vile and ignoble. I surely did.

He smiled at me, a genuine natural smile like Agio's. His eyes were really there. His face was not straining. "You're wrong," he said. "No creature is nobler than the human being."

I protested. "As a doctor who has delivered children, vaccinated children, mended and medicated children, most of whom are now slaughtered and buried in unmarked graves – how can you honestly say such a thing?"

Still shining a soft light on me with his eyes, he said, "I used to think our struggle was between good and evil. But when I got older I realized that the good have clay feet, and the evil are persons in need of healing. The real struggle, Rama, is between faith and despair."

That night I was awakened again. Someone indeed was haunting me. I shouted. No reply. My blood pressure was up. But, unlike the previous two nights, I eventually fell back asleep. I dreamed...

...Somehow I had collected all the blood shed in Africa during the 20th Century. I had also collected all the blood shed on the other six continents during the 20th Century. I had a blood bank as large as a city.

I heard leaders of tribes say to their tribesmen, "The blood our comrades shed was costly, but that is the price of Belonging."

I heard leaders of democracies say to voters, "That is the price of Freedom."

And others say, "That is the price of Socialism."

And still others, "That is the price of Peace."

And when I heard how costly was this blood in my bank I felt happy. What great assets I possessed!

Then I saw the angel of the twentieth century appear at the door of my bank. He said, "This blood is all infected." And I knew it was, and I fell into despair.

Not because of the blood, but because of the sacrifice.

I despaired because of the sacrifice – the noble giving of beautiful people who died for our nation, for our freedom, for our rights.

That sacrifice, and all the pain that went into it, was for nothing.

"Waste, waste, waste," I screamed as I woke up.

The bed linen was drenched in sweat, and I was cold. I looked at the wall clock. Its face was the face of Agio... a smiling, affable face with a word of hope for me.

It was time. With longing in my soul, the phone in my hand, I dialed green. "Agio, I must meet you. I must look at you... Yes, yes, tomorrow, the arboretum."

Nairobi Arboretum, Morning, January 5, 1999

Rama, Wasomaji, March 4, 2000

The morning was dark. Huge thick clouds moved slowly over our heads in an eastward direction. It was 7:30 but dawn had not yet dislodged the night. Patches of the night lingered in the clearings. We sat down on a park bench in the small clearing on the hill where people sit to watch the mugumu trees. Agio chose the spot. He knew every tree in the arboretum and the advantages of each of the park benches. He leaned back now on his favorite bench, clasped his hands behind his head, and said, "Beautiful."

"Listen, I can't wait a minute longer, Agio." He turned to me, smiling, and placed his hands under his thighs so the palms were touching the damp green bench.

"What is it, Rama?"

"I had to see you, er, well, I mean I had to see your eyes." His skin was wrinkled and warm. He didn't resist. I held his head and studied the light in his eyes. "How can you have those eyes at your age?" I asked. He laughed. His eyes sparkled even more.

"That, Rama, is a story for another day." He removed my hands from his face. Then he clasped my head between his bench-moist hands. I pulled back. "No, let me see," he insisted. I gave in. He studied my eyes. "Where has the light gone?"

"That is what I want to tell you, Agio. I must tell you... My work, I mean the blood bank, it's gone bust. It's been bust. And my insides, the fire, whatever, it's gone out. Drowned. Imagine the manager of the Central Bank reading in the morning paper that the shilling has been devalued by 100 percent. The guy's broke, busted, you see. Do you get the point?"

I felt he didn't. I wasn't sure what he knew. But I was bursting; I had to tell it all.

"We received reports of a virus discovered in the United States which destroyed the immune system. That was the beginning of the eighties. By the middle of the decade we had identified the same virus in some of our blood donors. It was always hard to get blood donations. Now we couldn't accept blood from some of the willing donors. The donor supply was tainted. And from then until now, as the years went by, less and less of it was HIV-free.

"In December 1998 one of my senior staff came into the office. He looked agitated. Without sitting down he told me the bad news. Certain procedures had not been carried out. This is what he surmised. Because, he told me, a large quantity of HIV seems somehow to have gotten into the blood stored in our bank. I exploded, 'Gotten into?' The man explained to me what had happened. It's a complicated and technical story, too lengthy to tell you now. But the fact was that we were storing hundreds of gallons of useless blood. We were bankrupt.

"On the spot, I decided to resign, but, then, the following day, I reconsidered. Out of despair I got a second wind. 'Nothing matters anyway,' I thought. It surprised me to think that thought, but I realized that I had in fact given up the very day in 1984 when I first heard of HIV. That day the Quixote in me started dying. Yes, I knew then, fourteen years before my senior assistant said it, that this would happen. The despair grew in me year by year and it slowly strangled Quixote. At the end of 1998, Quixote was dead. What remained was a phony – a phony wishing not to be a criminal."

My body was shaking; I was cold, very cold. I knelt down against the park bench. I held Agio's hands, "Forgive me, please, please, forgive me. I am sick, sick with it, the guilt and despair. I want to be well. Give me back the light. Give me back the innocence to smile as you do. Absolve me, Agio, absolve me."

Agio held my hands and told me to say the act of contrition. He started it, "Oh my God, I am heartily sorry..."

I continued, "For having offended Thee and I detest all my sins..." As I continued a downpour came. Thick dark clouds burst. The rain pounded us. "...Who art all good and deserving of all my love..." I finished. I waited. Agio leaned down and shouted in my ear, to be heard over the torrent,

"You're washed, cleansed by the blood of the Word."

Agio's Place, Early evening, 2 February 1999

Rama, Wasomaji, March 11, 2000

"Sit, sit, come, let's sit."

"Where?"

"Here on the carpet," said Agio.

Barefoot, Agio stepped onto the carpet and wiggled his toes on the soft threads of the thick Persian carpet. He sat down and into the beautiful green. He leaned back on his arms and stretched his legs forward as the Kikuyu women do when they rest in the grass.

Standing, stalling, I said, "Who made this carpet?"

"Lwanga."

"But I didn't know he was a weaver?"

"Oh yes," said Agio. "A very good weaver. And Lwanga had his reason for weaving. When he gave me this carpet he told me his reason. He explained the significance of carpets."

"Tell me."

"The Coastal People, the original Swahili, believed that the first created thing was a carpet. And the carpet was spread on the throne of Allah. After sitting on the carpet for a few billion heaven years, Allah begins to imagine the universe."

"Uh, huh, what's the point?"

"The point is that Allah did not rest on the seventh day after working for six. Allah rested before creating and while creating. Allah was sitting, and at leisure, probably day dreaming, when from the carpet all the forms of creation stood up."

"So that's what Lwanga told you?"

"Yes, when he came here to help me spread this carpet."

"I notice he wove an ibis in the middle of it, and I'd say that's a yellow cassia the bird is perching on?"

"You're right, Rama. Now come sit down beside me."

What could I do? I had stalled long enough. I sat down.

After a few minutes, once I looked comfortable, Agio said, "Rama, you made a confession and were forgiven in the arboretum. Now I will give you the penance."

I turned on my side to face him, "Penance?"

"Yes, take these greenbeads, your penance is to do one green day a week."

"A green day?"

"Once a week you must enjoy Nairobi as it is and not think of improving it."

"A day off. Well I can do that. There are many entertainments in Nairobi."

"I'm not talking about entertainment," said Agio.

"Then what is there to enjoy?"

"Enjoy Nairobi as a child sitting in the temple."

"Ah. The Fifth Green Mystery?"

"Yes," said Agio. "The Moslems and Animists understand it better than we Catholics."

"How so?"

"Take a Moslem for example. He carries his carpet wherever he goes. You've seen him. He always travels with water kettle and a carpet – whether he's traveling to Wajir by lorry, or to Marsabit by camel, or walking down a street in Majengo. He is prepared for five ritual washings, and five sittings. He reads the sun which signals the sacred times and he spreads out his little carpet wherever he is."

This Agio... what an innocent, I thought. *He knows nothing about evil and suffering in the world, and he considers himself educated. The simpleton. He's not a guru, he's nothing but a nursery teacher.* And that's how I saw him as he continued with his speech – a cross legged nursery teacher lounging on a green ibis carpet giving instructions about sitting and other nursery ABC's.

"Now the pastoralist," Agio was saying, "He gazes at his cows for hours. He sings love poems to his favorite. Be he Maasai, or Turkana, or Rendille, or Pokot, he carries a headrest and he knows the peculiar joy of a headrest. With it he can lie down and gaze better at his favorite cow, at the concrete details of that beloved cow - skin coloration, spots, marks, shape of horns, and other body features. The animist plays with these details in his mind until that one particular cow becomes luminous with suggestive implications about the universe, and our place in the universe. The cherished cow for this cattleman is the philosopher's stone, a cipher, a gospel. Out of a cherished particular come the universals."

"And what does any of this have to do with my penance?"

"Your cow is Nairobi. Once a week you must look at it. Don't assess it, quantify it, plan it, or try to improve it, just look at it."

Annunciation – Rama's Recitation of His First Lesson in Joy, 25 March 1999

Rama, Wasomaji, March 18, 2000

I arrived a half hour early. I stood outside on the bottom step for a few minutes and I tried to remember the last time I was at City Market. Then the scenes came back to me – the sellers and the stalls of the sixties. As a boy I used to go to market on errands to buy fresh fruit, vegetables, spices, meat, eggs, fish. Each seller was called by his or her produce – Mama *Ndizi*[4], Mama *Viazi*[5], Baba *Pilipili*[6], Baba *Nyama*[7], Mama *Mayai*[8], Baba *Samaki*[9]. Standing on the first step of the market I remembered each of their faces and the way they handled their merchandise: how Mama *Viazi* would select the largest potatoes from her huge sisal gunia and would bang them against the cement floor to knock off flecks of Kiambu clinging to its progeny, and how Baba *Samaki* with his bloody hands would grab from his steel sink a tilapia by the tail and would slap it against the wood block and slice off its head with

---

[4] *Ndizi* – Bananas.
[5] *Viazi* – Potatoes.
[6] *Pilipili* – Pepper.
[7] *Nyama* – Meat.
[8] *Mayai* – Eggs.
[9] *Samaki* – Fish.

his sharp cleaver; and how all the sellers would wrap up my purchases in day old newspapers and how even those papers would sound fresh as they were folded to fit the shape of bananas, or tomatoes, or a cut of lamb, or a dozen eggs.

As I walked up the remaining steps leading to the entrance of the mammoth three story squarish building and saw the life-size ibis carvings standing under the market's verandah I remembered the day I visited the tourist section of City Market. It was a wondrous day: I had held Kisii soapstones, and I had held musical instruments from various tribes, and I had played on a goatskin drum pretending I knew how to play.

When I reached the top stair I passed by the fish stalls and entered the ground floor of the spacious market chamber. I sat down on an empty *kibau*[10] next to a *jiko*[11] where a kettle of tea was steaming. The market chamber had three levels, all visible from where I sat. Fruit and flower vendors mostly occupied the ground floor. I could smell the wet green cuts of flower stems and the oranges. The next two floors were for the tourists. That is where Agio and I were to make our tour. A tour of the first Joyful Mystery. Right!? What a strange man this Agio. Fifty-two years old and still excited about looking at the stuff in City Market. What was he doing with me? What had any of this to do with the weariness I felt?

After sitting on the *kibau* for a few minutes I pulled out of my pocket Agio's green beads and fingered them. I didn't want to look at the market things. I had no desire to gaze at all the color and shapes presenting themselves to me in that chamber. Nothing appealed to me as it did when I was a boy on errands. I had no connection to these things anymore.

At the end of the first decade, I heard his salutation. "*Salamu*[12]!" shouted Agio walking behind a slow moving flower

---

[10] *Kibau* – Low stool.

[11] *Jiko* – Charcoal burning stove.

[12] *Salamu* – Hail (Ave).

vendor laden with a large barrel of silver pink Gabriel Trumpets.

Agio took me by the hand and we ascended the stairs to the second floor. We passed by the gourds, the batiks, the masks, the embroidery, and the leather products. We went straight to the bead crafts. Then Agio selected three different bracelets. "Look," he said, "at the color pattern of this one." The beads were alternating white and black. "Read it, Rama. What does it say?"

I shook my head, "I don't know."

His green eyes sparkled, "Mount Kenya, of course. The Maasai call this pattern, *'keri'* because the bracelet's alternating bright and dark colors connects the viewer to the white glaciers and black valleys of 'Ol Donyo Keri,' or Mount Kenya.

"Now this one," said Agio. He held a bead bracelet with a more striped pattern. "What does it say?"

I took it in my hands and looked at it. "Well, I see lines of blue and white running parallel to each other... but that's all I see."

Agio took back the bracelet. "These stripes of blue and white are called *'engoitiko'* and connect the viewer to the animal, *engoitiko*, or zebra."

"And what of this third one," said Agio. "How do you read it?"

I took it and held it close to my eyes. I said the first thing that came to mind, "You've seen the savannah sky right after a rain shower, well, to me, it looks like that."

Agio laughed and clapped his hands. "You got it! The pattern is named *'Sampu,'* and brings joy. *Sampu* can also appear in the skin coloration of a cow and brings rain to mind during the long dry days when the *sampu* cow is praised in poems and songs."

Agio returned the three bracelets to the saleslady and we stood outside the bead craft stall and leaned over the railing so that we could see the three levels of the great market chamber. "Wearing beads makes one a book," said Agio. "When a man or woman wears a bead necklace they connect me to lofty mountains, galloping zebras, promising skies... They link me up, they tie me in, they make me a part of it all."

I looked at the colors and patterns in City Market, and said, "The various bead patterns help people to recognize nature repeating herself – this and this are like that and that."

Agio smiled. "Yes, if you're willing to read them, beads mediate relationship; they connect one thing to another."

We lingered there at the railing. Neither of us spoke for a while. I gazed at the flower vendors below carrying in more Gabriel Trumpets and wondered what kind of beads the Archangel was wearing when he visited the maiden of Nazareth. And then I had an even stranger notion of her going up and down the lanes of Galilee repeating to everything she saw, "Hail thou full of grace," beading one thing to another using the original pattern of things that she alone knew. I didn't want to forget what I was thinking so I wrote it on the bus ticket in my pocket.

Visitation – Rama's Recitation of his Second Lesson in Joy, 31 May 1999

Rama, Wasomaji, March 25, 2000

Agio asked me to meet him on May Thirty-first at the National Theatre. It would be my second green day. I arrived a half hour early and sat down on the theatre steps. I gazed at the giant eucalyptus trees waving at me from a field between the theatre and Uhuru Highway. I took the greenbeads out of my pocket and fingered them. My mind wandered.

The plot of Eucalyptus near the National Theatre is where the Nairobi Train Station once stood. The trees had watched over the comings and goings of Africans, Indians, and Europeans. And, as Lwanga used to say, trees know every language since every language is printable on paper.

Those station trees must certainly have gotten an earful. Scores of African languages were spoken and thought under those trees; scores of Indian languages were spoken and thought under those trees; scores of European languages were spoken and thought under those trees. What stories did the trees overhear from those many varied people coming? What stories, I wondered, did those trees overhear from those many varied people going?

The people coming: stories in the offing, stories made of dreams; many stories of anticipated success, stories in the heads of emigrants from India's Gujurart as they stepped off the train at the grand station of the capital city. I thought of my grandfather as I handled the green beads. What story was in the mind of my grandfather when he arrived in Nairobi? What was he telling himself as he stepped off the train? What hopes? What dreams? What feelings did he have under these Eucalyptus trees? What fears? What desires? I wondered about this. I knew that he had great expectations, and a powerful hope, my grandfather. He and thousands of other Indians arrived at the turn of the century when they called East Africa the "America for the Hindu."

The people going – what stories did they leave with? Ernest Hemingway left from this train station. He had slept at the Norfolk Hotel, fifty meters further up theatre hill. Karen Blixen left from this station after the death of Finch Hatton. She went to Denmark never to return to Nairobi. She went with stories, many stories, delightful stories out of Africa. Theodore Roosevelt left from this station with heads of rhino, and lion, and tusks of elephants, and his hunting stories. Winston Churchill left from this station to tell Whitehall stories about the swampy un-hygienic capital of British East Africa. So many stories left this station. The station building has been torn down, and the tracks taken up, all that remains are the trees, guarding in silence the stories they overheard in their youth.

I had never thought a lot about my father. I preferred thinking about my mother and her side of the family, the immigrants from India. But sitting there on the theatre steps near the former train station reminded me of a story mother once told me about father.

Mother told me that father came to this station from Kisumu. He came to work as a cook in the New Stanley Hotel. When he got off the train he was taken by rickshaw to the New Stanley. Being a famous chef, by then the most coveted cook in the colony, his arrival in Nairobi was made much of. The New Stanley paraded their prize in that rickshaw through the streets of Nairobi and paid boys to run beside the rickshaw shouting: "Here is the greatest chef in East Africa and his unforgettable dishes can be tasted at the New Stanley."

Mother told me that father loved to watch people dance. She told me how he would get the kitchen workers dancing after work at the New Stanley. He'd wait until the bosses were gone and the mopping was done and then he'd pull out his drum. Mother enjoyed describing the scene to me. Under the eucalyuptus I could almost hear a whisper of her voice telling me...

...And then your father switched off the kitchen radio and from behind the cast iron stove he pulled out his drum.

He played it with vigor, with flat palm and knuckles, and the waiters kicked off their shoes and they danced in the New Stanley to Luo beats.

Your father was considered the best drummer in Nairobi. He loved the drums and the stories of the drums. He wanted the "*ngoma*[13]" to be released from the *ngoma* and possess the dancers. He was a happy man and he wanted happy spirits to possess the dancers.

He was a singer too. He sang the stories, the funny stories. And his voice was sweet as his baking.

No man alive took as much pleasure in the passing show as did your father..."

---

[13] *Ngoma* – The same word means "drum" and "the spirits of the dead."

"Rama, Rama!" The noise woke me from my daydream. It was Agio with his hand out to greet me. "*Habari gani*[14]?"

I answered, "*Habari yangu ni nzuri*." And I felt my news was *nzuri*, it was fine. The great things I had remembered somehow exalted my soul.

We went inside the theatre and took seats in the middle row. The lights dimmed and a reader appeared on a low stool. He had two file folders. From the first he took old headlines from *The Nation*[15]. He read to us about famine and war and terrible diseases for two minutes. He looked up and asked, "How many of you stop there?"

Then he took old Bouquets and old Watchmans[16] and human features from the second file folder. He read to us about kind people who opened their houses to displaced persons during the bad days of the land clashes. He read to us about a kind woman who rescued a newborn child from the ditch, of the kindness of young people to old people, of the kindness of farmers to their farm animals, and of the kindness of savannah people to wild animals. He read about beautiful deeds, and the beautiful, marvelous creatures who did them. And after fifteen minutes the man stopped reading and stood up and walked off the stage and sat in the audience. From his seat he said, "That was to prime the pump, now I would ask others in this auditorium to stand up on stage and tell us of other moments when Nairobians were caught doing something RIGHT."

After a few minutes an old woman went up front and climbed on the stage. She said, "During the election riot in Korogocho when the Moslems were being killed by the Christians, there was a Catholic priest who called the faithful to church and said, 'If you are going to kill people wearing these Moslem *kofias*, then kill me

---

[14] *Habari gani* – How are you? Literally, "What's the news?"

[15] *The Nation* – Kenya's largest daily newspaper.

[16] *Bouquet and Watchman* – Columns in *The Nation* reporting good things people do.

too.' Then he took a *kofia* out of a big box and placed it on his head. The faithful were quiet for a while. Then, one by one, they came forward and took *kofias* from the big box and placed them on their heads. With so many Christians looking like Moslems the riot soon ended because no one knew who to kill."

Similar stories followed: stories of good deeds, of funny events, of happy things; all celebrating the beauty of human beings. The stated theme of "Stories Centennial" was "*Watu Wazuri, Juu, Juu*" which, roughly translated, means, "Up, Up, With People!"

During the intermission Agio and I sat on the balcony bar at the end facing the Eucalyptus trees. He ordered a glass of dry cider. I ordered a Tusker. "Cousin, " I said, "those stories were nice and refreshing but..." I didn't go on because I saw he was grinning at me. I had pleased him by calling him cousin on the 31st of May[17].

I lost the desire to finish my "but" phrase. He didn't hear me start it anyway. He sipped his cider, smacked his lips, grinned some more and said, "But did you hear a difference between the newspaper stories and the verbal stories?"

I knew what he was driving at, and at that moment I didn't mind letting him take me there. So I said, "The newspaper narratives were English and the verbal narratives were Swahili; the English stories, of course, were missing the *Ka*-tense."

Agio loved to talk about the *Ka*-tense. Now I had given him his chance.

"Yes, Rama. In Swahili when someone puts "*Ka*" in front of a verb you know you 're entering the story world. The stories we just heard really happened. But *Ka* can also be used for fictional stories."

"Yes, it is the way fiction is done in Swahili," I said. "*Ka* gives the hearer permission to suspend disbelief."

"*Ka* is the magic 'what if,'" said Agio. "It makes an adult

---

[17] *May 31* – Feast of the Visitation of Mary and Elizabeth.

audience listen like children. When you hear *Ka* before a verb you are allowed to suspend your doubts. Then anything can happen. Fairies dance. Animals talk. Trees walk. And bad people really can become good."

I sipped my beer and looked at the Eucalyptus trees. I disliked this *Ka* stuff when Agio had published it as an article in the *Wasomaji*. But I listened. For some reason I didn't mind it that evening.

"You know what, Rama? I think you would not be so glum if you put *Ka* before your deeds, I mean, in your mind, when you're telling yourself that you're doing something – I am now immunizing the two hundred and fourth child in this school at 11:05 am' - tell it to yourself in Swahili and in a story way, with *Ka*. It puts you in a story that always makes sense. In story, nothing is there that doesn't belong: A is always followed by B, and you trust what follows next is C; the Doc vaccinates, the child is immunized, you see results. That's *Ka*-consciousness. Mind it, Rama."

I said that I would try. I put down my beer and looked at the trees.

Agio asked me, "Do you know how *Ka* is used in *Shang*[18]?"
"No. I don't use *Shang*. Adults aren't supposed to."

"In *Shang*," Agio said, "*Ka* is not only used with verbs, it can also be used in front of English nouns. *Ka* makes those nouns look a little ridiculous. *Ka* on an English noun is like nappies on grown men. *Ka* before a noun diminutizes the thing.

"*Ka*house means a funny little house. *Ka*bus is a funny little bus. *Ka*problem is a funny little problem. In translating '*Ka*,' one may, in place of funny little, use 'so called' as in *ka*guardog, the so-called guard dog (maybe you're talking about a Chihuahua). So *Ka* is not just for narrative, it also, at least in *Shang*, puts humor into things. *Ka* lightens the English noun.

"Lwanga often used *Ka*," said Agio. "He called it the 'jester

---

[18] *Shang* – The Kiswahili slang used in Nairobi, especially by young people.

tense' or the 'cartoon tense.' He used to tell me that the body has a funny bone and language a funny tense. He often reinforced this point with an Italian proverb, "Without humor nothing is serious.'"

I put down my empty glass, wiped my face with a paper napkin, and gazed long at my "cousin." He was always consistent in his naiveté, even coherent.

He went on. "*Ka* is for laughter. There is a time in a man's life when he must return to laughter. *Ka* puts a funny face on the sad one, a clown face let's call it. Smiling, one begins to think that one has a reason to smile. Work is not oppressive then, it is *Ka*work. The burden is not heavy then, it is *Ka*load. And failure? It doesn't make one give up. *Ka*failure is so-called, only seeming to be so."

Agio stood up to go back inside for the end of the show. He said, "*Ka* is to language what a comedy mask it to theatre. It signals to the audience, 'It' s OK to laugh; for sanity's sake, you've got to laugh.' *Ka* is the tense of play, the tense preparing one for a punchline; it is the same as a wink. With that tense I'm telling you, 'Isn't this job crazy? Admit it - in a *Ka* context, this work is damn funny - so for heaven's sake, let's laugh about this *Ka*job.'"

I got up without a word and followed him inside the theatre. When we sat down in our seats before the lights dimmed Agio asked me if I had ever read Zorba the Greek. I hadn't. He said that I should. I said I didn't read books any more. He told me that at the end of Zorba the Greek, after spending lots of time and money on building a pulley system to transport logs down to the railhead, and after the whole thing collapses in front of him on the same day it is officially blessed, Zorba breaks out laughing and begins to dance.

That's just fiction, I thought, and I was irritated. *What does Agio want me to do? Dance when I think of my* Ka*bank?*

In the second half of the show Agio got up on stage and said, "I know about two cousins of old, but really of all time, who were, the both of them, pregnant. They lived in hard times under the weight of a colonial monster. The one cousin said, 'God in me will bring down the *Ka*mighty, and lift up the lowly; God in me will feed the hungry and send away the *Ka*rich.' Then the other cousin said, 'Happy are you because you've conceived the tense.'" Agio sat back down next to me. No one else in the theatre understood what he was talking about, but he had achieved his purpose. He leaned over, smiled at me and said, "I can't speak the Magnificat without *Ka*."

After the show ended and we were on our way to the bus stage, I let out my frustration. "Agio, you have a *Ka*mind, a funny little, so-called mind."

I knew this was a misuse. *Ka* is not for satire, it's never used with a sneer; *Ka* is for jesting and is used with a wink. I was threatened and I wanted to insult Agio, but the silly man let it go, he chuckled politely as if I didn't mean it.

Rain had moistened the ground while we were in the theater and there were flying termites everywhere. Agio pointed at a cluster of them and said, "Look how badly the termites fly with their new wings – those ill-fitting wings, those *Ka*wings! Do you think, Rama, that maybe the termites should stick to the ground instead of making themselves ridiculous? They do look ridiculous looping upside down, crashing into things, winging themselves in that crazy uncontrolled way. After all, they only have those wings for two or three minutes before losing them and dying. Wouldn't it be better if they just crawled into the ground and died without this seeming exaltation? It's a lie really. They'll never fly in a correct manner. Why does rain give the termites those *Ka*wings?"

The bus arrived. I wished Agio well until the next green day. I didn't know what else to say.

I was quiet the whole way home. I didn't even speak to the passenger next to me. But I wasn't quiet because of anger. In fact, I was feeling happy – an emotion I noted as strangely exotic. I was indeed quiet in bus 46 that night, but not noiseless. Every now and then I chuckled at my *Ka*self.

Nativity – Rama's Recitation of His Third Lesson in Joy, December 1999

Rama, Wasomaji, April 1, 2000

I cancelled the next meeting and the one after that. In the month of July a child had died from a transfusion of HIV-infected blood. In the month of September two children had died from the same thing. When I phoned my senior assistant about this he told me that the blood had been from Martyrs.

When we destroyed our supply at Martyrs Blood we thought we had done so in time. We were wrong. Three transfusions had been released a few days before we had burned the tainted blood. Neither I, nor my senior assistant had been told. It was given to children who had been in a *matatu*[19] accident. The night attendant had been beseiged by distraught parents. After two hours he was finally persuaded and he provided KNH the blood although it had already been condemned.

The night attendant was too frightened to say what he had done. But after the death of the three children, he admitted that he had released the blood. This is what the senior assistant told me.

With the death of the three children it became impossible for me to face Agio. In Agio's company I had started to read joy back into life. I had even thought of reading a book. Agio's stories had begun to change me in May. But the moment I heard about the children I saw Agio as a deceiver, duping me. I did not want to be near him. At least that is the way I felt for the rest of 1999.

Agio let me alone until the end of the year. In the first week of December he phoned me every day asking for an appointment. Finally he prevailed. He said we should meet at the abandoned bookstore on December 25th.

I arrived a half an hour early and sat down on the steps at the front door. It was eight in the evening. Holidaymakers were not to

---

[19] *Matatu* – Minibus used in Nairobi for public transportation.

be found in the streets of Nairobi on Christmas night. Everyone was in their upcountry home, on the family farm. City Hall Way was deserted. The night was cold and clear and I could see a few stars above City Hall. The building seemed much kinder in the starlight.

After a few minutes I took the green beads out of my pocket. Since my confession in the arboretum I'd fingered them daily. I remembered my last meeting with Agio at the National Theatre. His words about *Ka* had made me happy. Thinking of *Ka* reminded me of stories. One in particular had played over and over in my mind, the story of Mama Warthog. Lwanga loved telling it to me. He animated it with the movements of a warthog while lecturing it with an Oxford accent: "Consider the lowly warthog…"

I saw Agio turn the corner. He was carrying two stools, a table drum, and a shoulder bag. I went to help him. He greeted me and said he had everything well balanced, but if I could just open the door? He gave me the key. I took it and opened the door slowly. Agio said, "Get in now. Come on. It's cold outside."

After arranging the drum and stools near the window of the chat corner we both sat down, and looked across the drums at each other. Agio said, "Just like it used to be, eh?"

"Not quite," I said.

"Lwanga is not here, but let us still do December Festival, tonight. What do you say Rama? It's Christmas you know. In my bag I've one book, I'll remember enough of the others…"

I kept quiet.

"Fine, let's start. The best way to open the December Book Festival for 1999 is with Ibilisi."

Agio stood up and walked to the middle of the empty room and said in his theatre voice, "Of course we all know the story of Ibilisi. A proud angel was he. But he wasn't proud in a wicked way. He was proud of beauty. He wanted to safeguard the beauty of divine worship. He could not accept a human being in the celestial choir. That ugly creature would detract from the angelic liturgy."

Agio flapped his arms making himself out to be an angel, "*Glooriaa, Gloooriaaa, In Excelsis Deooooooo.*" He laughed at his own mimicry until seeing my poker face he went on with the story.

"Well, uh, yes, now where was I?"

"Ibilisi, the perfectionist," I said sullenly.

Agio straightened out his "wings." "Yes," he said. "Only fallen angels are perfectionists."

"Isn't God in heaven a perfectionist?"

"On the contrary. Perfectionists live in hell." Agio paused a moment and then continued the story.

"As we know, Ibilisi was outraged when God asked Adam to sing with the angel choir. Ibilisi refused to sing with Adam. He rebelled, he and many other angels walked out, or flew out, or somehow vamoosed out of heaven in disgust. Ibilisi claimed that Adam was not worthy, Adam was not beautiful enough and so…"

I cut him off, banging the drumtable, "Wait, wait!"

Agio sat down cross-legged on the floor in the middle of the empty room. "Yes?" he said with that *Ka* look in his eye.

"Ibilisi was right." I touched my head, my chest, my buttocks, my feet. "Adam is not beautiful enough."

Agio uncrossed his legs, pulled a knee up to his chin, and flapped his eyelashes. "Tell me, Rama, tell me, why not?"

"Take the *Ka* from your eyes, Agio, and you will see the world as it is: Children die of hunger, man and woman at war, tribe killing tribe, nation against nation.

"It goes on and on. And the damnable thing is that we've got the solutions in our head. We know the social and medical solutions, but we lack the will to carry them out. Adam lacks the courage. Adam has beautiful thoughts, but it ends there."

Agio started tapping the ground. He tapped a dance rhythm. "Rama, do you know this step?" He played it again slapping the floorboards with his open palm.

"Yes," I said. "It's the beat used to call up the ancestors at the beginning of an evening dance."

Agio played it a third time. "*Ngoma ni ngoma,*" he said. "The *ngoma* or drum is the voice of the *ngoma* or ancestors. When the *ngoma* hear the beat they possess the dancers. It is the ancestors in the dancers dancing the dance. And Rama, it's they who dance in us – this dance of our living."

I didn't get the point and must have made a funny face.

"Rama, be careful," said Agio, "when you judge Adam not beautiful enough. You offend the ancestors." Agio played the dance again beating his soft hands against the hard floor. He waited and looked around the room, as if expecting someone to appear. Then he continued in his lecturing voice, "To say that God's creatures cannot express beauty is sinning against the holy ghosts of our beloved dead."

"Yes, yes." I screwed on a smile. "And now tell me, Agio, that it's the only unforgivable sin. Aren't I right? Of course I'm right! I know my catechism too." I patted myself on my back, "An 'A' student in CRE standard five[20]."

Agio chuckled, and we both laughed out loud.

After that the old bookstore seemed all the more quiet. A few eternal minutes later Agio took a book from his bag. "This is Lwanga's December Book. I want to read a story from it, if I may."

I didn't respond. He read anyway.

> The girl was only fourteen. She looked more innocent than fourteen, but at the same time more experienced than fourteen. She was younger than tomorrow and older than the dawn of time.
>
> When the angel came into the room the girl was sitting. She wasn't doing anything in particular, maybe flipping through a book. She was enjoying her

---

[20] CRE – Christian Religious Education Standard five – Fifth Grade.

leisure.

Then the angel said to the girl, "Do you see that children are hungry, that husband and wife battle, that nation wars against nation?" The girl admitted sadly that all the angel said was true.

"Suppose," said the angel, "that you were able to remove all the suffering in the world by carrying out one, only one of God's requests. Would you?"

"Of course," said the girl. "Take my body and let it be burned, let it be whipped, let it be cut with knives, I'd willingly accept pain of any kind to better the sorry human lot."

"What if," said the angel, "God's request was not as you describe?
What if you could better the human race by a simple 'yes' to the beauty there?"

"I am ready to do anything," said the girl. "What do I have to do?"

"To do?" said the angel, smiling. "Just Be That Yes."

Agio closed the book.
"So simple, eh?" I said sneering. "Say yes to our Beauty. Of course, so, so simple." I puckered my lips and threw him a kiss. "Thank you, great teacher. That's the point, the point of the human race. Be Beautiful! Of course! How could I have missed it?"
"Yes," Agio whispered, recoiling. "It is the point however

ridiculous it seems to you."

I didn't say anything, I couldn't; I was alarmed by my satirical outburst; I was frightened by the cynicism living in me. Poison snakes and hairy spiders and nail-toothed rats were scurrying around in my chest.

Agio spoke a little louder. "What do you think of that, Rama? What if? What if following that one request could change the world?"

I didn't answer him. I pulled back the tattered curtain and looked through the window at the stars shining above city hall. They were laughing, but not at me, not at us. The stars, I realized for the first time in my life, are not cynical.

My face was pressed against the windowpane. Yes, the stars were laughing. Not because human acts were worthless in the cosmic economy of cause and effect. No – stars are not cynical. Something else made them laugh. What?

I put both hands on the glass where, seven years ago, Lwanga had taped the notice for his final March festival. And through the glass, searching the heavens, I saw "What."

The stars were laughing at a child wetting the hay of a manger. And what's so funny about that? Well, look at it from the stars' point of view: these stars, these mighty stars that can spin planets in a circle, who owe their existence to the Big-Bang-Maker, see the All Powerful, the commander of the Universe, unable to command a baby's bladder!

"But why did God do it?" I wondered aloud.

"Why did he do what?" asked Agio.

"Why relinquish command? Unless – unless that was the more beautiful thing to do. And God chose to do the more beautiful thing. Now, now, that changes my image of beauty."

"As it did for Ibilisi."

"Who is beautiful then?"

"The Imperfect! Beautiful are the poor, beautiful are the sorrowing, beautiful are the meek, these are first in the reign of God."

Then it broke out – I couldn't control it – crystal laughter, pure star-like laughter.

"That's the point!" I said, clapping my hands. "When God becomes as imperfect as beatitude, Christmas happens. The human race is saved by this, saved by beauty." Then I screamed with all the power of my throat and lungs, "Ibilisi, do you get it? Saved by imperfection, by Beauty!"

Tapping the glass with my pinky, I went on, "Hey, Ibilisi, that's letting go, eh? That's getting pretty, do you hear me Ibilisi! To be in charge of everything, to control it all, and then, poof, the next moment, you can't even control your urine. That's Beauty!"

Laughing again, I farted. I couldn't control the gas.

"Are you okay?" asked Agio bewildered.

Turning to face him, I stopped laughing, and said, "Forgive me, brother, for insulting you at the grave of Lwanga; I sinned against you and against the ancestors, you are all Beautiful, and I beg all to green me... How did you put it Agio? The mantra? Hmm,

"*Urembo wa*
Ulimwengu
Thou, Chlorophyl,
Flow green in me."

Nativity Continued – Rama's Continued Recitation of His Third Lesson in Joy

Rama, Wasomaji, April 8, 2000

(The two Readers still sit in the chat corner of the abandoned bookstore. Here is what happened next.)

"I don't read anymore."

"I didn't say to read it."

Agio handed me the December Book.

On the cover was the hieroglyph for Thoth, a letter shaped like an Ibis. I flipped through the pages looking at pictures of the Arboretum, the City Market, the National Theatre. I also saw

Lwanga's illustrations for Swahili translations of *The Wind in the Willows*, *Peter Rabbit*, *The Wizard of Oz*, *Alice in Wonderland*, *Peter Pan*, and *A Christmas Carol*. Then I came to Lwanga's green version of African fables. There were talking birds, wise spiders, clever rabbits, and of course, lizard and chameleon. I held the book open a moment at lizard and chameleon.

Agio tapped the page and said, "Please read that one."

"I don't read anymore," I again replied.

Agio took the book from me and started to read:

> Chameleon was sent by *Ngai*[21] to deliver a message to the first man and woman and the message was this; "The Child shall not die but live forever."

(Agio was reading in the *Ka* tense. This famous story about immortality had lots of *Ka*.)

> Lizard, whose message was the opposite, "The Child shall die and never live again," ran faster than the daydreaming Chameleon. Lizard was the likely winner.

(I had heard the story a thousand times, but I listened carefully to the end this time. I found myself hanging onto *Ka* as Agio read how chameleon *Ka kimbia*,[22] and lizard *Ka kimbia*. My future, it seemed, and the outcome of this race were the same thing.)

> "Just before reaching the finish line..."

Agio stopped reading and looked up at me. He placed the book

---

[21] *Ngai* – Kikuyu word for God (The Great "I AM") who lives on the snow covered top of Mount Kenya.

[22] *Kimbia* – Run.

on the drumtable still open to the finish line.

I looked at Agio, begging him with my eyes.

He looked out the window.

Having to know about the Child, I swallowed and cleared my voice, "Finish, Agio."

He ignored me.

I looked long at the December Book, and at its green cover.

I sighed or moaned or groaned, how can I describe the air that came out of my lungs? It was like the ghostly bellow of the sacrificed ox at the moment when it finally collapses to the ground. That's what came from my lungs as I let go of myself and read the December Book of Lwanga.

> Though chameleon lost the race that day,
> and lizard told the first human beings
> that the Child would die and never live
> again, *Ngai* was not defeated. *Ngai* chose
> a better messenger.

> *Ngai* sent a pregnant virgin to recent
> human beings and she gave the right
> message, the truth.

"A pregnant virgin? Wait a minute," I said, putting down the book. "Why did you replace the chameleon with a pregnant virgin?"

"The messenger of God appears as a pregnant virgin," said Agio. "In the New World, at Guadalupe, Mexico, she appeared as a pregnant Indian Virgin. In the Oldest World, at Kibeho, Rwanda, she appeared as a pregnant African Virgin. The color of a chameleon, the color of the true messenger, is evoked by its environment."

I picked up the December Book and continued reading aloud. "The pregnant virgin sent by *Ngai* is a sign to the world." I looked up again.

"Isaiah, the Christmas Prophet," said Agio. "And this shall be a sign to you: the Virgin will be with child."

"A pregnant virgin is the sign?" I asked and shrugged my shoulders. "But I don't get it. I can't read it!"

"That's the challenge of joy," said Agio. "God sends a pregnant virgin as the sign and says, 'Do you read me?'"

I picked up the book again, and, a bit reluctantly, read:

> A pregnant virgin was about to give birth and the red dragon, Seducer of the whole world, waited beside her that he might devour the child once it had been born.

I stopped again and looked up, "Book of Revelation, chapter 21."

"Yes," nodded Agio. "The *red* dragon always waits to devour the child." He looked at me and asked, "Who do you think that lizard, the red dragon is? Who's the seducer in your world?"

I was quiet for two or three minutes but I had to admit it. "Ibilisi!" I said. "The one who refuses to accept that a human form can contain the Divine Word. I think he is the red dragon."

"The seducer who would devour the *emerald* child," said Agio.

I looked down at the December Book. I had a strong desire to read more, but soon I looked up and said, "It stops there." I closed the book feeling sad. "There are no more words."

"Here is a word," said Agio. He handed me an egg! "Read this."

The moment Agio placed the egg in my hand I felt something crack in me. And then, well, then, I shut my eyes and said, "Help me be reborn."

Agio sat down and moved his chair close to me and said, "Lwanga once put an egg into my hand and told me to read it. He told me that the Word, the primal sound through which everything was made is the word, '*Kraaack!*'"

Cracks formed at the edge of my closed eyelids. One small tear appeared in the crevices by the right eye.

Agio continued, "The inexorable power, the hatchling force."

The tear was now large enough to roll down the side of my face. It was only then that I knew I was crying. I put my hand to my cheek to touch that tear, the first one to escape my body in twenty years. "There is something in me that cannot be contained any longer," I said.

"What is it?" Agio asked.

I opened my moist eyes and almost giggled the word, "Wings."

Agio smiled.

I repeated the word, "Wings." And I laughed out loud, and then found myself wiping a flood of tears from my eyes.

Agio took the December Book from me and flipped ahead to the last page of it. "Read this," he said. "It is a continuation of that text from the Book of Revelation. We use it in the mass of August 15th the feast of the Glorious Assumption." Agio placed the December Book on the drumtable in front of me and pointed out the text.

Still holding the egg in one hand I put my other hand on the December Book and moved my finger under the words: "And the dragon released the flood of raging water, yet, behold, the woman is given wings, the wings she needs for flying through the night, for the night-sea journey."

"Have you ever heard of the term, '*Capax Dei*?'" asked Agio.

"No," I said with my finger still pointing at the word "wings."

"It is a term used to describe the pregnant virgin. It is a gift I was given, a gift for you, Rama. Lectio it."

"*Capax Dei*," I said. "'*Capax*' is capacity. '*Dei*' is God." I paused and said, "*Capax Dei*: Capacity for God."

Agio remained silent.

I repeated the phrase, "*Capax Dei*." I paused again and lowered my head on my chest. I closed my eyes and it seemed as if I were looking down my throat and into my heart. Then I said, "Capacity for the Uncontainable."

"Say the words to yourself, over and over, as a mantra." said Agio.

With eyes still closed I did so: "*Capax Dei, Capax Dei, Capax Dei...*"

"Use this mantra through to the end of the century. Yes, until the end of this week."

I opened my eyes and said, "Thank you for the Christmas gift, Agio." Then I stood up and stretched my arms out wide, lifted my hands as high as they could go, and said, "Wings!"

Agio looked at me and said:

> When you have come to the edge of all the light you know,
> and you are about to step off into the darkness,
> faith is knowing one of two things will happen:
> there will be something solid to stand on,
> or you will be given wings.[23]

Still standing with arms outstretched a verse came to me. It was the last stanza of the Christmas Carol, "*Gloria in Excelsis Deo.*" I sang out:

> Hail the heav'n-born Prince of Peace!
> Hail the Sun of Righteousness!
> Light and life to all he brings,
> *Ris'n with healing in his wings.*
> Mild he lays his glory by,
> Born that we *no more may die,*
> Born to raise us from the earth,
> Born to give us *second-birth...*

"Tell me about these wings. What are they?" I asked.

"Reading!" said Agio. "The capacity to read both sides of everything."

"I had one wing, but I could not fly with one wing."

---

[23] A quote from a book whose name Agio could not remember.

"Yes," said Agio. "You were able to read all the sorrows in the world. You were able to stare long and hard at death. But that was only one wing, until today."

"Until I reached the edge of all the light I knew."

"And," said Agio, "At the edge you saw the end of the end."

"And it makes me feel giddy with a strange new hope."

"Lectio this," Agio handed me the text which follows. "It is a good way for us to end this Christmas mystery. It was written by G.K. Chesterton when he was doing lectio on the Christmas parties in the novels of Charles Dickens, where old men and old women dance joyously with merriment in their eyes."

> It is currently said that hope goes with youth, and lends to youth its wings of a butterfly, but I fancy that hope is the last gift given to man (sic), and the only gift not given to youth. Youth is preeminently the period in which a man can be lyric, fanatical, poetic; but youth is the period in which a man can be hopeless. The end of every episode is the end of the world. But the power of hoping through everything, the knowledge that the soul survives its adventures, this great inspiration comes to the middle-aged; God has kept this good wine until now. It is from the back of the elderly gentleman that the wings of the butterfly should burst. There is nothing that so mystifies the young as the consistent frivolity of the old. They have discovered their indestructibility. They are in their second and clearer childhood, and there is a meaning in the merriment of their eyes. They have seen the end of the End of the World.

The Twelve Days of Christmas 1999 – Rama's Recitation of His Third Lesson in Joy, Part III

Rama, Wasomaji, April 15, 2000

Leaving the bookstore I decided not to go directly home. I wandered downtown and read everything – the stop signs, the shop signs, the billboards advertising Handel' s "Messiah," "Reggae Nativity," and Lux soap. I walked down Kenyatta Avenue and then Muindi Mbingu Street to University Way and then, via Moi Avenue, returned to Kenyatta. If I saw a newspaper blowing in the wind, I chased it and jumped on it with both feet and lifted it up under a streetlamp and read it – classified ads, weather, news, sports, stock indices, and parts of the newspaper I didn't know existed. My desire for reading was insatiable.

Through the entire week of Christmas I visited bookstores (the libraries were closed) and bought green novels, green poetry, green travelogues, green biographies. I didn't know there were so many green biographies. I read the lives of singers, dancers, and fairy tale makers. Lying open on my kitchen table near the animal cookies, were the lives of Beatrix Potter, and the VonTrapp Family.

My mind was swimming in *Ka*; my head was full of birds and flowers and everything bright and beautiful. I was looking forward to telling Agio what had happened. We had arranged to bring in the new century together at his flat.

Thus I found myself in Agio's sitting room at seven pm on New Year's Eve. He was still out, so I took the opportunity to peruse his bookshelf. O'Henry's *Story of the Magi*, something I'd considered sentimental piffle, made me happy, without rereading it, just holding it in my hand. I laughed as I remembered the two lovers giving to each other what they most cherished only to discover their sacrifice for each other had rendered their gifts to each other unusable. "But the uselessness of the gifts did not make the love less real," I said out loud. Opening Agio's other books, I began to hum the tune of *Greensleaves*.

Finally about ten pm Agio walked into the sitting room. He saw O'Henry lying on the coffee table. I said I liked the twist in that story and that I wanted to write an essay with a similar message.

"Call it, 'The Montfort Move,'" said Agio.

"What?"

Agio took off his jacket, put on the tea, and cut me a slice of Christmas bread.

"With all you know about Mariology you aren't familiar with Grignon de Montfort? He lived in the eighteenth century and told his followers to let R. G. Marie distribute all graces they gained by charitable deeds. Montfort's thinking is strange, but fascinating. It goes something like this – giving material goods to the poor, a soul gains spiritual goods for itself, but this gain might make a soul selfish, so R. G. Marie was to be given the spiritual goods so that she could distribute these to needier souls."

Agio placed a tray with the sweet bread and hot tea on the table and we began to eat and drink. "Do you see, Rama? The spiritual goods gained by acts of charity do not depend on that charity's success, what matters is one's desire."

"My bankrupt bank has gained me a lot of graces," I said, laughing.

"Let R. G. Marie distribute your assets," said Agio, not laughing.

"Are you saying that unsuccessful love is not waste?"

Agio put his hand on mine and said, "Love is often unsuccessful, doctor, but it will never go to waste."

"If placed in the hands of R. G."

"That's right. She is the Distributrix."

"I feel like going back to work. Do you think I'm ready?"

"Yes, Rama, and remember: *nothing is wasted; nothing matters. Nothing – what at present you can not perceive – this nothing matters most, in the end.*"

Glory, Glory – Rama's Recitation of the Glorious Mysteries, January 2000, Eastlands and Kenyatta Hospital

Rama, Wasomaji, April 22, 2000

The director of the city health department hired me back into the immunization section. I asked him not to make me an administrator. He obliged, and appointed me to the mobile vaccine team that went out into the neighborhoods of Eastland.

At one site, Ngeto, a young mother, presented her one-year-old boy – I think we were doing measles that day. The child was so thin and I thought he must be HIV-infected. There was a long line of patients and I didn't have the time right then to counsel this mother so I asked her to wait a moment in the consulting room. An hour later after I had finished vaccinating some fifty children I went into the consulting room. The young mother was seated, crying. She was trying to suckle the infant though he couldn't even hold up his head. She did this for him, bracing his head and placing his lips right up against the nipple, but he didn't suck hard enough to draw the milk out.

One week later this baby was dead. He died in Ward 22 at KNH where I referred him.

I have nothing more to add here about how we can prevent such deaths through our child survival campaign (the importance of clean water, proper nutrition, vaccine, etc. is well known). Instead I would like to speak of a strange incident that happened to me the day this child died.

Under a thevetia tree, seated on a bench across the street from the hospital morgue, I ate a mango from my paper bag lunch. I was reconsidering Agio's advice. Why had I come back to this kind of work? The children were still dying. More were dying in fact. Despite our vaccination efforts more and more children were immunodeficient. The photo of the blood dumping came to my mind, and the words of Agio, too. He had disagreed with me when I told him that the sacrifice of all those people had been for nothing.

Lunch finished, I wrapped up the paper bag and put it in my pocket. I was just about to stand up and go when an ibis alighted above me in the thevetia. It was making the "Ha Ha Ha" sound. That irritated me. What do these creatures have to laugh about so near the hospital morgue?

Observing the bird more carefully I noted it was carrying something in the talon of its right foot. Squawking again, the ibis flew away dropping the object. It fell on the bench and I picked it up. It was a round green seed.

For whatever reason I put that seed on my string of red beads. (I still used Red on the job.)

Everyday for the next week, I found myself seated on that same bench thinking the same thoughts after news of more deaths in Ward 22. It was a mistake to follow Agio's advice; how could *Ka* stay in my head when my eyes were misty with grief?

But each time doubt came to me an ibis would also come and drop another round green seed on my bench. My passion rosary now had five decades of eleven beads, the eleventh were all green.

At the end of the week, instead of taking my lunch under the thevetia after the usual bad news from Ward 22, I decided to get out of there and take a walk through town. As I was reading the beads I began to meditate on Nairobi...

In my mind's eye, I climbed into a *matatu*[24] and walked past the driver to the back of the van. At fifty-and-a-half, my eyes were not as good as they used to be, but I couldn't believe that they saw an ibis sitting in the driver seat.

The *matatu* pulled away from the curb. It passed city center and started on the number nine loop through Eastlands. "Oh damn, I'm on the wrong bus!" I muttered to myself.

I decided to wait it out knowing I'd be back in city center in twenty minutes.

As I looked out the window I saw Juja Road had changed. In place of the mud shanties there were handsome stone houses in

---

[24] This daydream of Rama has been illustrated by schoolchildren attending schools along the Route of Bus Number Nine; Rama had several of these "Ibis at the Wheel" drawings framed and hung them on the Wall of Ward 22 at KNH.

green yards with trees and flowerbeds. I rubbed my eyes.

When the *matatu* tout[25] came I had my shillings ready not wanting any abuse. The lad smiled at me and asked if I was comfortable. He shook his head when I held out the money, "No one pays on the number nine," he said.

Puzzled, I looked back out the window. We had made the turn at St. Theresa's and were headed down Eastleigh First Avenue. I didn't see any street children. There were plenty of children all right. But they were dressed in clean bright clothes and were playing in schoolyards. I must have seen four schools before we reached General Waringi Street.

What was going on?

And besides all the other marvels I hadn't used the handgrip, to save my head from hitting the van ceiling. Could it be that we hadn't gone through any potholes or over any speed bumps?

As we were passing by Bahati, which was as beautiful a neighborhood now as Mathare, I got up from my seat and went forward to the front seat and sat down next to the driver.

The ibis turned to me and asked if I was enjoying the trip.

"Sure am," I said. "But could you please explain something to me?" The bird nodded. "Where did the city get the resources to change these neighborhoods?"

The bird laughed, "Ha, Ha, Ha." But I was persistent. "I really don't know. Tell me, please, who paid for all this?"

At that point we were headed down Landhies road and were almost at the end of the trip. The bird shifted into a lower gear and said, "Been told it has something to do with four thousand, two hundred fifty four people who donated blood in the eighties; don't know how it works, but they paid for what you see."

Getting off the *matatu*, I found myself seated under the thevetia holding my rainbow rosary. Smiling, I said to myself, "I know how it works."

---

[25] Tout - The conductor on the minibus (matatu) is called a Tout; he is the one who collects fares and shouts out the stops of the bus route. These lads are often tough characters.

Editor's note – Liberita

The following texts were never published in the Wasomaji, but they have been taken out of our office files for this section of part Three (Confessions) because these texts will help you understand better what was happening inside Rama when he changed and began the unmapped, daring journey of the second half of life. With the author's permission then, we are pleased to present a poem and three journal entries of a doctor who has made it through the midlife transition.

Woodbeads

Rama, 2000

My beads are wood
In wood green is made.

I finger the wood
and attain green peace.

I finger the wood
and rest on the branch.

My beads are wood
In wood green is made.

I read the wood
and attain green peace.

I read the wood
and rest on the branch.

My beads are wood
In wood green is made.

In green I'm remade.

A Lectio of Cracks

Rama Journal 12th June 2000

Emerson, a great reader, once said that everything in God's creation has a crack in it. This is true and has always baffled me. I now understand that the cracks in everything serve a purpose. It is how grace gets in.

I have decided to remove the awards and citations on my office wall and replace them with my baptismal certificate and a sermon by Rev. Tillich, which Agio gave to me. Beneath those testimonials of grace I will display one more. I am going to ask a few of my fellow Readers, those who've faced their imperfection, to lectio the texts below and choose the truest.

A lucky wind it was
— The luckiest possible —
That blew off my halo.
Thomas Merton

*Actual Grace is the beauty that draws us to the plough handle, it is the burst of energy we anticipate from the door-handle every morning when we open the shop door. **Redeeming Grace** is the mercy that washes us when we come from the field or close the shop door; it is the voice of Jesus that saves us from despair when we put down our needle or paint brush and surveying our precious work realize the action taken is very imperfect; it is that voice from the cross which says "Your offering is accepted."*
Lwanga

The path of human development begins with innocence (paradise, childhood, the irresponsible first stage). From there it leads to guilt, to the knowledge of good and evil, to the demand for culture, for morality, for religions, for human ideals. For everyone who passes through this stage seriously and as a differentiated individual it ends unfailingly in disillusionment, that is, with the insight that no perfect virtue, no complete obedience, no adequate service exists, that righteousness is unreachable, that consistent goodness is unattainable. Now this despair leads either to defeat or to a third realm of the spirit, to the experience of a condition beyond morality and law, an advance into grace and release to a new, higher kind of irresponsibility, or to put it briefly: to faith. No matter which forms and expressions the faith assumes, its content is always the same: that we should certainly strive for the good insofar as we are able, but that we are not responsible for the imperfections of this world or for our own, that we do not govern ourselves but are governed, that, above our understanding is God, or Tao, whose servants we are, and to which we may surrender ourselves.

Herman Hesse

In the Shadow of Your Wings

Rama's Journal, 15 August 2000

On a red day in the casualty ward of Kenyatta Hospital I wrote down a daydream...

An ibis lifted me up and in the shadow of its wings I rejoiced. I was carried to the arboretum. There I was set down on a park bench. What met my eyes made me rejoice yet more.

I saw the park was full of people but not crowded. The people were reading. All of them were reading. Some read little green books. Some read large red books. And to my surprise there were many other book colorings – blue, yellow, brown, orange, and more.

An ibis, perched on the bench next to me, was clucking with contentment. I, too, did not want to change anything.

Gazing from where I sat I saw that all the Readers in the park were naked. The old people and the middle aged people and the young people and the children were reading their books in the buff.

And I saw that the bodies of the old people were whole and lovely. They were not bent or obese or misshapen in anyway. And when they moved – some did their lectio walking – their ambulation was gracious.

And I saw the bodies of middle-aged people were beautiful too. I saw no sign of stress or anger or heart failure. They were in fact laughing the laughs of innocents, and I did not hear any cynical laughter among them.

And I saw the bodies of the young people were smooth and clean and had no STD's or skin ailments. They were reading green poems and red technical manuals.

And I saw the bodies of children. None had measles. None had anemia. None had *kwashiokor* or *marasmus*. None had malarial fever. None were coughing. None were wasted. Some of the children were sitting in circles reading animal stories to each other. Some were sitting alone and reading of heroes and heroines. Seeing the children gave me the greatest joy. They were alert, well nourished, and healthy, all.

I thanked ibis for letting me see these beautiful readers with beautiful books under beautiful trees. I asked the ibis when in the future this would take place.

And the ibis spread its wings over me and said, "I cannot tell you. Only know this. What you've seen will happen. Suspend your disbelief. Rejoice in the shadow of my *Ka*wings. All will be well."

Loyal to the Multiform Me, a Changing Experiment

Rama's Journal, 2 November 2000

I am a termite with wings. I cannot claim to be a butterfly. Comparing the aerodynamics of a butterfly to that of a flying termite is like comparing the aerodynamics of the space shuttle to the Wright Brothers at Kitty Hawk.

I will never fly like the butterfly. My wings are not in sync. One flaps up when the other is flapping down. I turn right when I want to turn left. I go up when I am trying to land, and landing, gee whiz, I land upside down. Then it takes me an entire minute to get myself upright so I can take off again.

And those take-offs! My, my! They are not spectacular. I sort of jump and, hopefully, flap these disobedient wings enough times, in the right way, to get off the ground before the force of the jump is spent.

I am a funny sight!

But you know, even if my flights are jerky and swervy and short, still, my gratitude is unbounded – not for the expertise, not for the style, but for the *form*. That I can assume a new form, an unfamiliar, surprising form – this worm-with-wings form makes me high, higher than butterfly wings can, because *I'm in on the secret* – a secret about the universe. I know that form is not a restriction but an experiment.

Given that secret knowledge many things are now clear. I know why birds imitate one another's' song. I know why some trees borrow the form of others by wrapping aerial roots around their host. I know why one creature pretends to be another.

The truth is that only *Self* exists. And it is there in all forms and no two forms are so alien that they cannot interpenetrate; no two forms are so unlike that they are unable to imitate each other. Even the starfish without ever having seen a star – by the intuition of *Self* in the deep dark sea – has assumed the form of a star.

I've reached midlife. And I'm something patched together. Wings of bird, body of worm: I'm star-mud. But at every stage I've been something patched together: the baby with a big head and a small body, the teen with an adult body and a child's heart.

What a fabulous beast I am. A worm with wings! A composite.

I emerge from the prison of my old form, and put on new clothes, a new form, now that I am out. What a terrible wonderful thing to be free, to be *Self*.

And what wisdom, at last, I'm no longer ashamed of being human, a worm with wings, a crazy composite.

I've become "loyal to my imperfection" (J. Campbell); to the fabulous mixture of me. Yes, indeed, loyal to the multiform. Now, at midlife, I am devoted to the many, changing forms of me, to these temporary experiments of *The Eternal Self*.

Midlife Enantiodromia

Midlife Enantiodromia Introduced

Liberita

Naibis wanted to place here between the two confessions a word about enantiodromia at midlife. As mentioned earlier, enantiodromia is a yearning for wholeness: the desire in every thing to become its opposite. This yearning is at work in the whole creation at all times but is particularly strong at midlife, especially for persons who are at the extremities of a continuum such as the super-sorrowful or the super-joyful. Time comes for them to change; Kairos opens a door. And so we see with our Two Readers who at midlife seek each other out without knowing why. Naibis explains here that they do so in order to evoke in each other the opposite that lives in each of them, which until midlife was a phantom.

The Two Goals of Reading

Naibis

Many of you Readers say you want to be Guides. Then you'll need to know the two goals of Reading: Vocation and Evocation.

Vocation is gift. Evocation is responsibility.

Let me explain the first.

To read the text of the world and by this to make oneself readable - a new text, unabridged, singular, different – that is the first goal of Reading. That's vocation.

Look at R.G. Marie. She read until her flesh and blood became readable: Word. She was a younger woman then. Her role was vocation.

Now let me tell you about the second goal of Reading – Evocation. To be context, frame, background, field --- that is the second goal of Reading. That's evocation.

Look at R.G. Marie when her son was an adult. At Cana she was background and field. A single color page cannot be read. Without the relief of color, words on a page are not evoked, are invisible. The Word was made visible because R.G. evoked it at Cana. Mary was the page, Jesus the printed words. She was an older woman then, her role was evocation.

Evocative Reading

Carl Jung, the psychiatrist who "discovered" the collective unconscious, often described Enantiodromia with these words of the poet Holderlin:

> Where danger is,
> *There* the rescuing power *grows*.

For Two Readers I would say:

> Where danger is,
> *There* the rescuing power *glows*.

Where red fades, green glows brighter for the rescue.
Where green fades, red glows brighter for the rescue.

When the Readbead Leader comes to the edge of all the
reading he knows,
When the Greenbead Leader comes to the edge of all the
reading he knows,

That's when Lady Enantiodromia sends one to the other
As an evocative force, a hatching power, a rescuer.

Do you understand Rama and Agio? R.G. Marie sends into
your mono-color life a phantom that haunts you and haunts you
until you confess. Then, at last, you can begin to read the mysteries
of your otherself.

Confess, Rama! Hatch! See, Agio is cracking you open.
Confess, Agio! Hatch! See, Rama is cracking you open.

Come out *leisured* legionnaire!
Come out *activist* artist!

Let the power of the Evoker, the Egg-Cracker,
Help you to bring forth what must come out, for as Jesus
said…

If you bring forth what is within you,
What you bring forth will save you.

If you do not bring forth what is within you,
What you do not bring forth will destroy you.
The Gospel According to Thomas

Rama, let Agio help bring you forth. That Greenbead is your
midwife.
Agio, let Rama help bring you forth. That Redbead is your
midwife.

If you do not bring forth what's pushing to come out,

What is not born will remain a phantom and it shall forever haunt you.

Naibis
The Supplier of Evocative Reading.

Experiment in Evocation

Naibis

Biologists say that the color green travels on the same nerve-wire as the color red, just as blue and yellow use the same nerve-wire. What results?

The result is that the nerve-wire transmitting red cannot carry green at the same time. Each has a turn. One waits for the other.[26]

In the brain the complement of red is green just as the complement of blue is yellow. In the brain red and green don't unite to make red-y green or green-y red. Rather, one evokes the other.

Experiment with our book cover. Look at the black dot in the red heart for one minute and then look at a white surface, immediately green will appear. Similarly, red will appear on a white surface after you've gazed at green.

Have you ever wondered why green appears red on a film negative, and red appears green?

It is because:
Red is the phantom of Green.
Green is the phantom of Red.

---

[26] According to the Hering theory, red and green share a single coding mechanism. The after-image represents a switching of the codes, which were sent to the brain. The removal of the green stimulus causes the red code to be sent temporarily to the brain instead.

What Mary would say about Midlife changes

Naibis

The passion in termites is to grow wings
Odd?
Yes it is.
Termites are grubs that live underground. Like snakes. Haveyou ever dreamed of snakes with wings?

Don't shake your heads. Of course you have. They're called green dragons, magic dragons.

Now give me a chance to describe these airborne bits of mud that turn underground upside down.

They come out when it rains. Swarms of them come out of the ground. They've just sprouted wings and have no idea how to use them.

They flap around in circles on the ground a while not knowing that wings are for "up." And then, suddenly, some go up. It's a short flight like at Kitty Hawk and then crash, they go down.

Soon, the whole underground is trying it. Lift off, short flight dive, crash. The flying termites never get up for long. They bump against walls, and furniture, and people, and other objects in their path and then crash – they slide down the wall, the furniture, the people, and flap wrong side up on the ground, violently, until with Herculean effort they right themselves.

Aloft and down, aloft and down; that's the essay of termites.

Even if unobstructed, the termites swerve left and right, jerk up and down, as if their wings were loose. These wings never stop moving.

The wings are in constant vibration, each one out of sync with the other. I cannot imagine a worse example of aerodynamics.

But for all their impracticality, the impression given by the flying termites is unbounded joy. Though they crash and crash, swerve and jerk, land wrong side up, take eternity to right themselves, and still flap each silly wing separately; and though they're bizarre and airily absurd, the flying termites play out their final minutes of life, unlike humans with their serious midlife renewal programs, joyfully out of control, already in the mad ecstasy of unfamiliar form.

The mission, the daimon, of termites is to fly.

Ancient cultures saw in flying termites, moths, and butterflies something so mysterious and alluring that they fashioned gods in their image.

The Egyptians had their Scarab Beetle that rolled its ball of mud backwards and died and rose out of the mud ball, flying.

The Greeks had their Dionysus, the Romans their Bacchus. Dying, rising, flying gods. When I was at the side of the Creator giving my advice about the mission of things I recommended that everything have some termite *telos* in it.

When I was teaching the Redeemer about mission in Nazareth I advised him to look at each and every person with their wings in place, in their godliest image. I told him not to look at their failures but at their hopes and dreams: how they suspend disbelief.

When the church was looking for an icon of itself it used me. It pictured me as the good dragon flying over the evil dragon. You'll find the picture in the Book of Revelation. After the evil dragon, Seducer of the Whole World, is unable to devour my child, it vomits out a vile flood to drown me; but I rise above it with my wings.

Do you know what I've named my wings?

Imagination.

If you want to understand the mission of flying termites or the mission of people in midlife transition you have to understand that imagination is disdained by adults who get sober and serious about life when they start their careers; only when they tire of crawling careers do they look for the wings they left behind.

They've come to the edge of all the light they know by then. And it is usually dark and raining. Then, and only then, do drowning crawlers accept the termite daimon's offer of crazy wings, and learn, at last, to fly.

What a Mythologist Says about the Midlife Change

When one thinks of some reason for not going or has fear and remains in society because it's safe, the results are radically different from what happens when one follows the call. If you refuse to go, then you are someone else's servant. When this refusal of the call happens, there is a kind of drying up, "Acedia," a sense of life lost. Everything in you knows that required adventure has been refused. Anxieties build up. What you have refused to experience in a positive way, you will experience in a negative way.

If what you are following, however, is your own true adventure, if it is something appropriate to your deep spiritual need or readiness, then magical guides will appear to help you. Your adventure has to be coming right out of your own interior. If you are ready for it, then doors will open where there were no doors before, and where there would not be doors for anyone else. And you must have courage. It's the call to adventure.

A Joseph Campbell Companion, page 78

Confessions of an Artist at Midlife

Greenbeads Come Back

Agio, Wasomaji, January 22[27], 2000

I appeal to Greenbeads who refuse to pray the sorrowful mysteries to come back.

By itself, green is not honest.

Without red your green is veneer.

The day will come when unalloyed joy leaves you empty and dried up

Joy cannot stand on one leg.

Come back Greenbeads!

Be alive to all Nairobi. Befriend what's different.

If you only pray the joyful mysteries you will never attain glory.

Leisure without labor is false.

Sacrifice yourselves if you desire the deepest bliss. Learn to die if you would live.

Pray the red beads. Open your eyes to the suffering innocents. Serve!

You cannot be childlike without loving children.

---

[27] Feast of Fr. Chaminade, founder of the Marianists.

Greenbeads Come Back! (Preface to a Confession)

Agio, Wasomaji, January 22, 2000

Do I surprise you, Greenbeads? You never thought you would hear me say, "Come back to the Circle of Readers." But that is exactly what I am saying. Let us return and embrace the Redbeads.

Are you bewildered, Greenbeads? Are you asking yourselves, "What has happened to Agio? He is the leader of our faction, his green serenity inspires it. What has gotten into him? Why has he changed?"

To answer these questions I have written a Confession. It was a confession of a personal nature, a confession written for an old friend, Rama. But, at the request of Liberita and Naibis, I want the entire document to be published in the pages of the Wasomaji.

"Confessions of a Painter at Midlife" will appear in serial form during the first lent of the new century. I urge Greenbeads to read these issues of the *Wasomaji*.

If my confessions fail to reunite the Circle of Readers I will try something else. What more shall I do?

Should I go so far as to embrace Rama at the graveside of Lwanga?

I am willing.

Indeed, I'll do anything to have Greenbeads experience the healing power of loving opposites.

The Loss of Readers' Guide

Agio, January 29, 2000

Exiting Readers' Guide one day in February 1992 I saw Lwanga taping a notice on the window of his bookstore. It read:

Welcome to a Symposium for Nairobi Writers
Theme: Writing Books that Promote the Rights of Children
Venue: Readers' Guide
Date: March 25[28] 1992, 10 a.m.
Refreshments to be Served

"Redbeads will love that theme," said Lwanga pointing to the window.

"It's dangerous," I said as I walked nearer the door where he was standing.

"Why is it dangerous?" said Lwanga holding the door open for me. My arms were full of books about oil painting.

"What an innocent you are, Lwanga. Can't you see? Kenya is having its first multiparty election in 24 years; the government is nervous, the police are monitoring public gatherings, and here you are inviting CID[29]-tracked dissidents to join you for coffee and scones."

"An election year is the right time for these discussions," said Lwanga. "I hope the writers are from different parties, that way the symposium can hear the Action-Plan each party has for children. We must talk to each other to get the Nairobi we want."

"Please don't," I said touching his hand that held the door. Then I stepped outside and walked away.

Lwanga did not actually want trouble. He was not seeking arrest. He was hoping for a quiet discussion of the issues. That's why he only advertised the meeting in his bookstore window. But my hate for writers with a *cause* made me ridicule them in a letter to the Editor of the Nation Newspaper."

"Reading and Writing are for contemplation, not confrontation. When will the Redbeads learn this? Far better that they go to Church on the Feast of the Annunciation and read their beads there than foster rebellion in Readers' Guide."

---

[28] *March 25th* – Feast of the Annunciation, the day Mary became the Reader's Guide.
[29] *CID* – Kenya's Secret Police.

Those three sentences undid Lwanga's attempt to hold an inconspicuous meeting.

After the large gathering (of more than a hundred people) sang *Simama Imara*[30], Lwanga stood up and prayed to R. G. Marie to guide the discussion of "the Nairobi we want."

Lwanga stressed the word "we" by saying it more loudly. And just as he said the next word. "want," the police crashed through the door.

The police captain asked to see the permit required for public gatherings. Lwanga showed him. But the licensing officer had written the wrong date on the permit. That made it invalid according to the police captain. He arrested Lwanga and dozens of writers. Everyone was packed into a prison van. You know the kind, with the little wire mesh slits at the top that serve as hand grips for prisoners who have to stand up.

Lwanga lived in a cell for eight months. The air in his cell was cold because the window had no glass, only bars. The floor of his cell was always wet because of a broken pipe. And Lwanga got a chill from that cell he could not shake.

One visiting day, as I was walking down the prison hall, I spied Lwanga in his cell while I was still a distance away. I saw a bent-over, chest-infected man, hacking and wheezing, and nearly falling down.

I called out to him.

This sudden noise convulsed Lwanga in one long wheeze. He almost fainted from lack of oxygen. Then he straightened his tan beautiful body and moved toward the cell door, step by tiny step, holding on to a table and chair. Finally Lwanga got to the door. I wanted to hold him in my arms and carry him to the bed. I called for a guard to open the cell door. By the time the guard came, Lwanga was gasping for breath.

That incident prompted me to see the chief guard. I asked if the prison doctor could visit Lwanga. This was arranged. The

---

[30] *Simama Imara* – "Stand Firm," a popular hymn often sung in the shanty churches in the slums of Nairobi.

doctor gave Lwanga some medicine and modified his work regimen.

I visited Lwanga three times a week. I would go at times I knew Rama would be absent. I had no desire to see him. I hated my adversary more than ever. What had the Redbeads accomplished in their symposium? They had not celebrated literature. They had degraded it by making it useful. Rama and his Reds had desecrated Readers' Guide. This is how I thought at the time. My inside was twisted up with emotion. My love for Lwanga and my hate for Rama almost put me out of my mind that terrible November of 1992.

Because of his poor health Lwanga was permitted to leave his work duty (he was prison librarian) for fifteen minutes at noon to stroll in the hot midday sun. The prison doctor said this would dry up the drippings and heal the cough. A guard always accompanied Lwanga on these strolls.

The wound that sent Lwanga back home to his bookstore was incurred during one of those noontime strolls. Yes, it was that wound, in his thigh that got him sent home. Lwanga was released a month early because the thigh was not healing, and Dr. Rama convinced the prison nurse that the wound would never heal under prison conditions. Lwanga was put into the custody of Dr. Rama. The kind of care he needed made it possible for Lwanga to be cared for at home. The Ibisaji was happy when he got back to Reader's Guide.

Still Lwanga's condition worsened. The wound became dangerous. Then there were the days of fever.

I was with Lwanga at the last hour. I was sitting on his bed to comfort him.

But I was really hoping he would comfort me. I put my ear up to his mouth to listen.

Unfortunately what Lwanga said to me in his final breath gave me no comfort. A task was given me. I was told to read the glorious mysteries at his burial and to do this with Rama.

I did the opposite. I insulted Rama on that day even as Lwanga's body was lowered into the soil. I called him a violent man, an irresponsible revolutionary. I blamed him and his political party for Lwanga's sickness. I went on and on and I knew I was lying. Rama did not belong to any party. The presentation he had given at the symposium was not partisan, it was medical, "Women's Literacy: how reading has increased the number of immunized children in Nairobi."

I shredded his name and I knew I was lying. I didn't care. I wanted to hurt Rama. I loathed him and his activism and his detestable use of books. So I said what I said at the burial wanting people to see Rama the way I pictured him.

Lectio Leaves Me, Acedia Arrives

Agio, Wasomaji, February 5, 2000

After Lwanga's burial I was unable to pick up a book. I could not read, and I could not paint. My sleep was constantly interrupted. I was haunted at night with a song in my head. It was always the same song, *"Simama Imara."* It woke me up at least once a night. At times I also felt something in the room, a demanding absence.

Things did not go well for me. During 1993 and 1994, I became less and less an artist. My creative power was drying up. I was scared, confused. My life had been painting. Great painting. But when my paintings became mediocre, and fewer and fewer were sold, I was tempted by alternative careers.

Maybe I could do crafts? Sell to tourists?

Mr. X was an acquaintance of mine. He had a specialty shop. He called his products "Feathercraft."

Mr. X had found a niche in the market. Feathercraft competed well against batiks, soapstone, masks, and baskets. The tourists like pictures made of bird feathers. Mr. X had his three workers make scenes of beaches, forests, mountains, etc. The scene did not really matter. In feathercraft the most important thing was variety and contrast in the bird feathers.

At first Mr. X was satisfied with feathers that his workers found on the ground. But the growing demand for feathercraft products made it necessary for Mr. X to consider other ways, besides molting, to "mine" his raw material.

Mr. X never went himself to the arboretum. He hired street children and sent them. The boys went with their slingshots. They poached birds in Nairobi's sanctuary and in other bird parks and tree parks around Nairobi.

Mr. X thrived. He sold pictures in Paradise Flycatcher, Scarlet Breasted Sunbird, African Fire Finch, Rainbird, Red-eyed Dove, Olive Thrush, and the Cinnamon Chested Bee-Eater. Mr. X told the sensitive naturalists, who flocked to his store, that the feathers were only taken from molting birds or birds that died of natural causes.

I found Mr. X in his shop by the 680 Hotel. Mr. X was mounting some feathers on black construction paper. He used a fine, clear glue that didn't squash the fine fibers in the feather. He placed blue feathers by yellow and he made a beach. He placed green feathers by brown feathers and he made a forest. He placed gray feathers by red feathers and he made Mount Kerinyaga, home of *Ngai*.

As I watched Mr. X, I grew more and more uneasy. Was I now going to repudiate values I had held throughout my life, values about art, values about nature? Could I perform this devilish taxidermy? Did I want to dishonor the man I was, the man who loved birds, who loved the innocence of childhood. Suddenly I felt so tired. I was fatigued by the temptation. Some jinn or *shetani*[31] was assaulting the castle of my heart. Would I hold out?

At that moment a boy hunter came through the delivery door at the back of the store dragging a dead ibis. I fled.

The feathercraft temptation happened in 1993. I overcame that temptation, but I continued to dry up. This drying up I called acedia.

---

[31] *Jinn* or *Shetani* – Evil spirits.

Why me? I could not understand why I should be afflicted by acedia.

"Idleness" is often used as a synonym for acedia. But the sinfulness of acedia is not as "work-ethic-men" imagine. The sinfulness in acedia, according to Thomas Aquinas, is that one no longer consents to be a full self. One is overcome with sadness (*trisitia saeculi*) when faced with the goodness in oneself because the will to realize that goodness has disappeared.

In my case, when faced with the green in myself, I felt *trisitia saeculi* because my will to achieve green had disappeared.

Aquinas also says that acedia is a sin against the third commandment, a violation of Sabbath rest. One does not consent to be and become; one no longer enjoys being and becoming. One despairs of existence.

Thus acedia is the dry sin of restlessness. Acedia is the opposite of leisure.

To think that I, of all people, should sin this way – that I should sin against my own green soul, my self, Agio against *agio*.

It all started with a wrongheaded idea: leisure for leisure's sake. My goal was to paint with no goal, simply for the experience. That was a false green idea.

Jesus says that the Sabbath (leisure) is for "man" (e.g. human development), and nowhere in the Bible do we read that the Sabbath is for the sake of the Sabbath.

I understood my error. Intellectually I understood. My creative powers, though, did not return.

What could I do?

Heaven help me.

The March Book – April 1, 1994

Agio, Wasomaji, February 12, 2000

I did not want to go to the Edel Quinn Museum with its collection of red books donated by Rama. I did not want to see

Lwanga's March book either. The museum represented everything I feared and hated.

But one night during lent I had a dream, and I wrote down the rapid impressions of the dream:

> Surrounded by my late-period paintings:
> Colorful, Pure Form, Non-representational.

> An easel appears, and brushes and paint,
> But I am loath to reproduce the same.

> I am bored with playful colors and forms
> That are not recognized as anything.

> In frustration I push over the easel,
> And in its place appears a child.

> "Come and help us," she says.

> "Where are you?" I ask.

> "At Edel's place," she answers.

I was the only person in the museum – a one-room affair attached to St. Peter Claver Church. It had opened for the 50th anniversary of Edel's death.

Now it was Good Friday, 1994. How appropriate!

Seated in a chair, I looked about. I saw many books. Since Lwanga's death I hadn't read a thing, and had no desire to. Especially these books with titles and authors like:

Wretched of the Earth by Franz Fanon
African Socialism by Leopold Senghor
Weep Not Child by Ngugi wa Thiongo
Cry the Beloved Country by Alan Paton
The Legion History by Frank Duff

Minutes of the Children's Summit in New York
Women's Literacy: How Reading Has Increased the Percentage of Immunized Children in Nairobi by Rama

After an hour of staring at the red books I went over to the center table and stared at the March Book compiled by Lwanga. It was surrounded by Legion things like Edel's personal beads and the Vexillum of the first Nairobi Praesidium.

On the cover of the March Book Lwanga had drawn the hieroglyph for Thoth. Inside the book I saw the white and black feather of the Sacred Ibis. It was taped to the first page.

On the next four pages I saw sketches of the high trees. Lwanga used to call these the Utopian trees: Eucalyptus, Ash, Oak, Podo, Juniper, Cypress.

In the second section of the March Book there were illustrations Lwanga had done for Swahili translations of the Tales of *Narnia*, the Gospel of Mark, *Drumtaps*, and *Don Quixote*.

In the third section I saw newspaper clippings about heroic acts that Lwanga had collected over a period of thirty years. The clippings were pasted on the left page of the March book. On the right page Lwanga had sketched illustrations for each one. Several featured Rama. It's then I got frightened.

I closed the March Book, and with slow steps I backed out of the room.

Once through the door I turned quickly, and only then, with my back to the Edel Quinn museum, I ran willy-nilly for the bus stage.

An hour later, sitting in my studio, surrounded by pictures of colored joy, I was despondent. These paintings were not connected to anything. Emotion for emotion's sake, imagination for imagination's sake, art for art's sake. Pure, I boasted. Not propaganda like Rama's writings. I was a true artist, true as a child at play. Yet looking at my masterpieces that day made me despondent.

I thought of the Lwanga I had denied. His March Festivals, his March Book, his symposium for the cause. His passion and the red of him that had no part in me. I suddenly felt very tired. My head was heavy on my shoulders. I let it fall to my chest and I was asleep.

Another dream...

> I am in the arboretum gazing at an oak, towering high in militant ascendancy. A red eyed Ibis perches in the oak branches. In the beak of the bird is a red rosary.

> Beneath the tree appears a shelf of green books. I run to it and pull out a thick volume of essays by Josef Pieper containing *Leisure: the Basis of Culture*, and climb the oak.

> The Ibis doesn't fly away, and I crush its head with the full weight of *Leisure*.

I awoke with a start. I went to the window and flung it open. I looked up at the night sky and the shining stars.

"Leave me alone," I said .

But whom was I talking to? The dead Ibis? Lwanga? I felt stupid. I went back to bed, and fell asleep again and dreamed.

"Come and help us," said the child.

"Oh no, not you again," I answered.

The First Sorrowful Mystery – April 2, 1994

Agio, Wasomaji, February 19, 2000

Sitting in the darkest corner of the Edel Quinn museum, I thought of the dead Ibis and I wondered just how long I could wait before I'd have to bolt again.

PART THREE

161

After an hour a young girl walked through the museum door, straight on to the center exhibit, and bowed to the March Book.

Turning the pages of illustrations she nodded her head as if listening to the instructions of an elder. She hadn't noticed me in the shadows.

The girl went to the Redbead books. She took one from the shelf. I think it was something by Paulo Freire. She held it upside down and stared at one page for several minutes. Then she closed the book, placed it on the table, and sat down on the bench. She put her forehead on the book and started to cry.

I stepped out of the shadows and sat down next to the little girl. "Why do you weep?"

She was startled and sat up. Wiping tears from her cheek she asked in a loud voice, "Sir, would you teach me to read?"

"If you teach me the Red mysteries," I said, without knowing why I should ask this of the little girl.

The girl was actually fourteen. She looked younger than that and at the same time older. But her *kipande*[32] said she was born in 1980. It gave her name as Liberita.

This Liberita was more innocent than fourteen and more experienced too. She had been running the family household for a year. Her mother had died in June 1993, leaving Liberita responsible for the children: a twelve year old girl, and a baby not yet a year old. The last child was HIV-positive and often sick.

Liberita provided for these three children through the second hand clothes business she had inherited from her mother. That is where Liberita took me.

"The First Sorrow," she told me, "is the temptation in the garden."

"What do you mean?"

She smiled in the way an innocent fourteen year old would smile if she did not want to say the word, "prostitution."

Neither of us said anything for a while. We walked past the

---

[32] *Kipande* – Identity card.

Landhies Mosque and through a large crowd of *wasafiri*[33] at the Machakos Bus Station. Then I heard the shouting of the hawkers. We had reached our destination.

Kikomba market displays every stitch or clothing on earth. There are saris from India, Wranglers from the USA, chemises from France, leather shoes from Italy, bolts of red checkered cloth from the Philippines, and baseball caps from Mexico. Liberita told me that she specialized in shoes and chemises.

After we had passed by twenty or so kiosks we arrived at hers. It was made of second-hand *mabati*[34] like the others ten feet by eight feet. Inside, a little girl was washing up the breakfast plates. A baby boy was strapped to her back and he was bawling.

"This is Elizabeth, and this noise box here is Taak. We made his name up from a Maasai phrase, '*Taa A'Ke Iye*,' which is used by elders to bless newborns. It means 'Be Your Full Self.'"

Liberita took the bundle from her sister's back, kissed the crying infant, and whispered, "*Baas, baas*[35], it's okay."

The room fell silent as the baby nestled in big sister's arms. "We sleep on this side away from the stream," Liberita told me, "because there are fewer mosquitoes."

I looked at the polluted stream through the open window at the back of the hut. It did not have broken sufurias[36] and torn inner tubes in it like the streams of West Nairobi. The waters here were polluted instead by human waste, and by the one or two categories of the cow not eaten. The smell turned my stomach. I asked Liberita to show me how she displayed her wares. That would get me outside again. I needed air.

Liberita removed the shoes from a large plastic *gunia*[37] and handed them to Elizabeth. She carefully placed them on low

---

[33] *Wasafiri* - Travelers.
[34] *Mabati* – Iron sheets.
[35] *Baas, baas* – A phrase used to comfort crying babies. Like, "There, there."
[36] *Sufuria* - A cooking pot.
[37] *Gunia* - A sack, usually made of sisal.

shelves of plywood tilted toward the muddy road.

Ladies' shoes were bottom front, gentlemen's shoes were top back. I looked at the men's shoes. I actually needed a pair and tried on size eight. I removed them and turned one around. Under the toe was written "Italy." I said, "Oh, you are also an importer?"

Liberita smiled and said, "A man in Kariobangi makes them. He told me that they sell better when he writes those letters under the heel." I laughed.

"Well, I'd like to buy these. How much?" She told me they were three hundred fifty shillings. I gave her a five hundred shilling note. "Here," I said, "Keep the change." She looked at me with disapproving eyes.

"No," she said. "The shoes are worth three hundred fifty shillings. Take your change." She handed me one hundred fifty shillings. As she wrapped the shoes in an old newspaper she said, "Someday when I need a loan I'll ask you."

On our way out of Kikomba Market Liberita said, "I have my own business and it's a clean business. I don't go near sugar daddies. I don't want their dirty money. I don't even bribe the *askaris*[38] when they threaten to close my business down. The first decade of the red beads have made me an *Mshindi*[39] over temptation!"

The Second Sorrowful Mystery – April 9, 1994

Agio, Wasomaji, February 26, 2000

"Today we read the 'Crown of Thorns,'" said Liberita as we walked to Majengo. A week had passed since my visit to Kikomba and I'd used the red beads Liberita had given me to meditate on the first decade.

---

[38] *Askari* – Police Officer.
[39] *Mshindi* - Victor.

"This second sorrow mystery," Liberita said, "is about mind death."

Walking through Majengo I was propositioned by a sickly young woman, and then another and another – each one leaning against the wooden door of her mud hut.

The schoolhouse, a half fallen *mabati* shack, had no benches, no chalkboard, no pencils, no paper, and no books. And on that particular day, there was also no teacher.

The students were sitting on the wet ground fashioning statues of birds out of the mud. A twelve-year-old girl was supervising this activity.

The children stood up when I entered the room, and shouted in unison, "Good morning, our visitor!"

"Thank you," I said.

"You're welcome, our visitor."

Then they sang for me:

"I'm a little teapot short and stout
Here is my handle, here is my spout.
When I get all steamed up
Hear me shout:
'Tip me over and pour me out!'"

The twelve-year-old girl made the gestures as if the handle and spout were not her own limbs. She moved her body with a deadness that showed it was already detached from her soul. When she mouthed the words, "Pour me out," the vacancy in her eyes horrified me.

The Third Sorrowful Mystery – April 15, 1994

Agio, Wasomaji, March 4, 2000

The third meeting with Liberita was unplanned. Or perhaps I should say that I did not plan it, nor did she.

I was walking along Kenyatta Avenue and passed a vendor holding up the morning newspaper. The headline said, "Big Fire in Kikomba." I bought a copy and opened it to the article. There I saw a photograph of half an acre of smoldering *mabati* being cleared by a city council bulldozer.

"The fire destroyed everything," said Liberita. When I went to see the damage she was holding a long stick and used it to poke the cindered heels of her stock. Nothing else remained of shoes and chemises.

Elizabeth was holding the baby. She stared for a while at the ash heap and then at Liberita. Liberita took the baby from Elizabeth and as she did so she gave Taak a kiss on the forehead and said, "*Usikate Tamaa Mzee*[40]."

There was nothing to carry away. Liberita said we should say a decade of the rosary before leaving the ruins of her house and business. She selected the beads for "Jesus stripped of his garments." When we were finished, Liberita asked me for a loan of 300 shillings so they could rent a hut for one month. I gave it to her.

We left Kikomba and walked to Kinyago. "How did the fire start?" I asked on the way. Liberita told me the landlord was responsible.

"The landlord!"

She nodded. "You see, he needed us to clear out because he wants to put up a nightclub here. You know, a 'Day and Night Club.'"

I shook my head and clenched both my fists, exclaiming, "To sell children! To spread AIDS!"

Liberita looked at my pulsing hands. She touched them with her girlish fingers and said, "Convert this energy into action; red deeds free of hate."

---

[40] *Usikate Tamaa Mzee* – Don't let this break your heart, grandfather. In Kenya baby boys are often called "grandfather," and baby girls are referred to as "grandmother."

The Final Sorrowful Mystery that Almost Finished Rama – April 25, 1994

Agio, Wasomaji, March 11, 2000

I knew the call was from a payphone because I heard the coins dropping. One has to be fast with such calls to get the essential information before the line is cut. "Which ward, what time?" I said. She got the words out just before the busy signal began to beep in my ear.

When I saw Taak with the intravenous tubing in his hand I thought of the nails in the hands of Jesus. Not accustomed to making such associations I just stood and stared at the baby for a moment.

The tightness of his closed mouth. That is what struck me, the tightness. Why is it that extreme pain and extreme joy make us bite the lip?

I wanted to leave. This was the end of Taak. I didn't want to watch.

"Pathetic," I said as I turned to go.

Stepping quickly away from the deathbed I muttered, "Pathetic Kikomba child." I wanted to detach myself mentally as well as physically from the horror.

I didn't go far.

Liberita was standing at the door. "Thank you for coming," she said. But she did not ask me for anything, she did not say what she needed from me. I couldn't figure out why she had phoned me. I turned back to the child's bed and sat on a low stool.

Liberita put her hand on my shoulder and said, "I knew you would want to be here."

I touched her hand. "But I'm not a doctor. What can I do?"

"Be here," she repeated the phrase. "Be here and just sit a while."

(If you are familiar with the manner AIDS dehydrates its victim you have a good enough idea of how Taak died. I needn't go into the details.)

After the nurse pulled the sheet over the baby's head Liberita and I left the room. The nurse told us that the doctor wanted a moment to complete the death certificate that Liberita also must sign.

A few minutes later the nurse called us back. We entered the room.

There was Rama with his back to us holding the body of Taak. I stayed in the room only a few seconds – he never saw me – and in those few seconds I heard him pray, "*Uzazi*, inside me, I feel it, my red zeal, for…" He couldn't finish the mantra (which Liberita later taught me). Instead he moaned, "Oh God, why have you forsaken us?"

Liberita found me in the parking lot. "Why did you run away? I wanted to introduce you to Dr. Rama."

"It isn't necessary," I said. Then out of curiosity I asked, "How do you know Dr. Rama?"

"He is the one who immunized Taak," she answered.

"He works for the city council vaccination program, doesn't he?"

"Yes," she said, "But I doubt the city sanctions him giving rosaries to the mothers of the vaccinated."

"Rosaries?"

"That's right," she said. "Each mother receives a string of red beads and Dr. Rama shows them how to read them."

"Is Rama the one who taught you what you're teaching me?"

"Yes," said Liberita.

I went back, but did not find Rama in Taak's room. I found him in chapel near a Madonna Statue. He was saying:

When as a little child,
beset by smallest trial,
I went to Mary's shrine
I'd get some help divine.

Now in the middle years
with the usual fears

and a difficult job
I've come here to sob.

In this my darkest hour
when the great doubts devour
my youthful drive and hope
I've come again, help me cope.

Dear Lady, Queen of May
of youth, of flower, of day,
are you too Queen of Winter,
of age, of night, things less *douceur*?

Can I bring you my sloth,
My old lust, my deep shame?
Can I bring a heart cooled,
and smoldering ashes?

Will you understand me
if I no longer rhyme,
and my language is coarse,
without prettiness, rough?

Because that's how I talk
in the dark interval
in the time of great doubt
with a difficult job.

Queen of Winter, I know
you hear the dark voice too;
hear me, as you did your son,
who from the cross shared his doubt.

Rama didn't see me. I left him there in chapel. But I knew my responsibility. From that day on I watched for an opportunity to evoke the fading Redbead.

Glory! Glory! – Agio's Recitation of the Glorious Mysteries, Kenyatta Hospital

Agio, April 22, 2000

And suddenly a phrase broke through the eggshell of my mind. It had not been in my conscious mind for twenty years. But the phrase came to me right at that moment as if the words had been waiting for the right time and place.

Words do that. They suddenly appear when the listener is ready.

C.....? D.....?

C.....! D.....! *Capax! Dei!*

Capax Dei[41]! That is the phrase Lwanga told me to use for a mantra after I had finished with *"Urembo wa Ulemwengo."*

Capax Dei, or the capacity for every experience. Even for that which seemed uncontainable for someone like me.

And then, to my surprise, the twin of *Capax Dei,* climbed out of the same broken eggshell. I choked and said, *"Capax Novum.*[42]*"*

The inexorable, cracking-hatchling-force of the uncontainable was at work in me again. Just as at the arboretum when I broke out of my fear into a world of green Christmas, now at this hospital I was breaking out of fear again and into a world of Calvary-red-Fridays.

But Calvary-red was not as I expected.

I found that I had the capacity to live in a red world, the real world of pain and suffering.

This hospital ward is not a sunny place but now I've got mooneyes. I have the capacity to see by the light of hope.

---

[41] *Capax Dei* – is the Capacity for God traditionally ascribed to R. G. Marie who, for nine months, contained the Uncontainable. Agio considers his new Capacity for the Full Color Spectrum a glorious mystery. Ninth Month Theology is a kind of Marian Millenialism, a feeling of Hope, of Expectation.

[42] *Capax Novum* – Capacity for the New.

This hospital is not a place of bird song like the arboretum, but now I've got another set of hatchling ears. I have the capacity to hear a different egg crack.

The Word for all that is, for all that is here in this ward, sounds like an Easter Egg, sounds like the stone rolling away from his tomb, and, oh, yes, from my tomb.

Glory! For all that is here, Glory! For that Easter sun that I sense here – in the dark gloom of Taak's death room – Glory! I've made the midlife passage, I've crossed the threshold, and, at last, I've entered *a second, a clearer, adulthood.* Oh, what power I feel, and what passion, as I write and recite those two words: ***Sacred Adulthood!***

Editor's note:

Liberita

The following texts were never published in the Wasomaji but they have been taken out of our office files for this section of Part Three (Confessions) because these texts will help you understand better what was happening inside Agio when he changed and began the unmapped, daring journey of the second half of life. With the author's permission, we are pleased to present four poems and two journal entries of a painter who has made it through the midlife transition.

Glorious Ninth Month: *Capax Dei*

Written by Agio in the hospital chapel after seeing Rama beg R. G. Marie to rescue his red vocation.

Bigness.
A way of seeing, of feeling, of thinking.

Littleness
is not the way of R. G. Marie,
despite centuries of smallifications done to her
by humilitarians and simpletons.

September is R. G. Marie's month.

Hers the ninth month, she is full term:
Full Term seeing, Full Term feeling, Full Term thinking –
the way a Millenialist sees, feels, thinks;
ahh yes, I am in the final days too.

I am big:
I see big,
I feel big,
I think big,

And thus I become
big enough to contain
the uncontainable:
I am *Capax Dei*.

Uncontainable Word: Thou, Cracking-Hatchling-Force

by Agio

Burning up with hope,
Not realizing until now that hope
Is fire, an unbearable fire.

Emotions spontaneous
Heart pumping blood
Of Word made flesh.

Lifted up, like flames of high joy,
Not realizing until now that joy
Goes so high, so inconceivably high.

Busted in every blood soaked cell, by love
Not realizing until now that love
Grows so big, so uncontainable.

My body bears, conceives, contains, Thou:
Unbearable, Inconceivable, Uncontainable,
Thou, Red Joy: Oh, paradox! Oh, exuberance!

Red Word, to me, Thou art the Cracking-Hatchling-Force,
The inexorable annihilator of tame familiar forms
You have cracked me open,
Have risked me into wild unfamiliar form.

Preview of Glory
Written by Agio in the hospital ward where Taak died.

In the night it is the moon
which reflects
tomorrow's light.

In the night it is the moon
which gives us preview
of day twelve hours away.

Thus the names of R. G. Marie:
Capax Novum, Capax Lumen,[43]
Hope of Change,[44] Esperanza.[45]

---

[43] *Capax Lumen* – Capacity for Light.
[44] Mary's name in Hebrew (Miriam) means "Hope of Change."

Listen to the shouting moonbeams,
those light-rebels piercing the night:
"Change, Change, Change..."

(A message passed on from the sun.)

Moon, secret agent of Sun,
Mary, light of tomorrow;
May I be an agent, too.

A child lies dead in bed,
"The hungry will be fed,"
I cite you, Moon, light of tomorrow.

(Sightless in this death-dark ward, I cite you.[46])

"Magnify the Sun
With me," you said,
The Son lifts up the dead.

In our nights it is the moon
Which gives us preview
Of a new and endless day.

Ave, *Capax Lumen*!
Ave, Maria Luna![47]
Ave, Maria Esperanza!

Capax Novum *could also be described as the cracking-hatchling-force of the Uncontainable. That force is at work in*

---

[45] Esperanza – Often used to refer to Mary.
[46] Agio is citing Mary's words in Luke 1: 46-55, a seditious text usually cited by Redbeads.

[47] Luna or moon is an ancient symbol for Mary.

Agio. That force surging in him breaks the shell of a world too small for his bigger self, the fighter-artist. Alleluia! Hail Capax Novum! *Agio has changed, and so, now, he will be for Rama the rescuing power.*

In My Bonebeads I Make Blood

Agio

> My beads are bone
> In bone blood is made.
>
> I finger the bones
> and get red hot.
> I finger the bones
> and fire my work
>
> My beads are bone
> In bone blood is made.
>
> I read the bones
> and get red hot.
> I read the bones
> and fire my work.
>
> My beads are bone
> In bone blood is made...
>
> In red I'm remade.

Annunciation: A *Sympathetic* Imagination

Agio, from his journal

The secret of the rosary is what Walt Whitman called "Sympathetic Imagination." Or to put it another way, "What in the world is God up to? And how can I give a hand?"

Vincent Van Gogh in a letter to his brother Theo wrote:

> I feel more and more that we must not judge of God from the world, it's just a study that didn't come off. What can you do with a study that has gone wrong? If you are fond of the artist, you do not find much to criticize you hold your tongue. But you have a right to ask for something better. We should have to see other works by the same hand though; this world was evidently slapped together in a hurry on one of his bad days, when the artist didn't know what he was doing or didn't have his wits about him (letter 490).

Something has gone wrong, it didn't come off as desired. But what was God up to? This is Van Gogh's question.

How can you "dream the dream onward?" is a question Karl Jung asked his patients. "Dreaming Onward" is what you do in waking hours.

The Creator's dream, though it did not come off, was surely daring for the artist to have made the exquisite blunder we see in this sadly beautiful world. Van Gogh writes to Theo:

> "The study is ruined in so many ways. It is only a master who can make such a blunder, and perhaps that is the best

consolation we can have out of it, since in that case we have a right to hope that we'll see the same creative hand get even with itself. And this life of ours, so much criticized, and for such good and even exalted reasons, we must not take for anything but what it is, and go on hoping that in some other life we'll see something better than this.

Writing about Van Gogh in his book *Van Gogh and God*, Cliff Edwards describes the theology of the painter:

God is free to risk mistakes. For Vincent, mistakes, blunders, and imperfections, are the locations of hope. Blunders are the assurance that God acts with a self-forgetfulness that attempts more than can be reasonably expected or accomplished in the present. This confirms God's mastery and promises the success of his total "oeuvre."

Oddly then, the flawed universe, which is for many good people the cause of atheism, is the cause of Van Gogh's faith in God.

Edwards writes:

God, therefore, "must not be judged from this world," for its flawed and unfinished nature is our hope that the total work, the complete "oeuvre" has yet to be seen by us...

This expectation of "something better" to come, which emerges precisely from the fact of failure and imperfection, becomes for Vincent a kind of "proof" that there must be a more complete version of life than the "sketch" we experience, there must be a life after death with more favorable circumstances, and finally, there must be a God.

Praying the rosary is "dreaming the dream onward" toward "a more complete version of life than the sketch we experience" now. The rosary is an exercise in sympathetic imagination with the Daring Artist whose attempt at something better than possible gives us hope.

When we call the first mystery of the rosary "Annunciation" we put too much emphasis on what the angel did. I think it is misplaced attention. The angel's job was easy. The tough job was Mary's. She said "yes" to something better than was possible.

How many other young women going back 1.5 million years to the *Homo Erectus* we call Lucy (Eve?) were approached by this same angel and said, "No thank you."

What made Mary different?

I'll tell you. Mary's religion, the heart of all religion, is Sympathetic Imagination – a hunch about the universe. Through her reading of nature and scripture she got a sense of what God was trying to pull off and in sympathy for the grandeur of the "oeuvre" said "Yes, I will it, too. Oh, yes!"

The Plotting of an Evoker

Journal of Agio, December 1998

Doctor Rama is always quoting Emersion, "Everything in God's creation has a crack in it." The good doctor is right, but he needs to understand that's how the light gets in.

Ring the bells that still can ring,
Forget your perfect offering.
There is a crack in everything,
That's how the light gets in.
                    Leonard Cohen

Rama needs to understand that about the cracks and this about grace:

Grace strikes us when we are in great pain and restlessness. It strikes us when we walk through the dark valley of a meaningless and empty life. It strikes us when we feel that our separation is deeper than usual, because we have violated another life, a life which we loved, or from which we were estranged. It strikes us when our disgust for our own being, our indifference, our weakness, our hostility, and our lack of direction and composure have become intolerable to us. It strikes us when, year after year, the longed-for perfection of life does not appear, when the old compulsions reign within us as they have for decades, when despair destroys all joy and courage. Sometimes at that moment a wave of light breaks into our darkness, and it is as though a voice were saying: "You are accepted. You are accepted, accepted by that which is greater than you, and the name of which you do not know. Do not ask for the name now; perhaps you will find it later. Do not try to do anything now; perhaps later you will do much. Do not seek for anything; do not perform anything; do not intend anything. Simply accept the fact that you are accepted!" If that happens to us, we experience grace. After such an experience we may not be better than before, and we may not believe more than before. But everything is transformed. In that moment, grace conquers sin, and reconciliation bridges the gulf of estrangement.

                    Paul Tillich

I'll tempt Rama with the Chameleon story from the December

book. This is how I can start him reading again. Once he has resumed the practice, I'll have him lectio Tillich.

That's my plan. I'll phone Rama now and get an appointment. I've got to tell him a truth about the cracks in everything.

I must pray that R.G. Marie gives me wisdom.

Oh Red Lady Pieta, I turn to you
as Rama turned to the Green Lady, that Madonna
in the hospital chapel,
when his color was fading after the death of Taak.

Oh Pieta, help me to understand the sorrows of Rama
so I may lead him to those particular joys
that are genuine to his life.

Amen.

Part Four

Readings at a Wedding of Opposites

Liberita

After Rama and Agio reconciled with each other, they worked together to reconcile the Circle of Readers. But after more than two decades of division, this group they had previously worked so hard to divide resisted their joint leadership. They wrote articles for the Wasomaji, but the Readers boycotted the newspaper. They appealed to Readers individually and in groups to recognize their other half, but with limited success.

Finally, Rama and Agio arranged a "Wedding of Opposites" to be held at Lwanga's grave. They wanted to fulfill Lwanga's final wish, a reconciliation at his own funeral. Rama and Agio personally invited twelve of the Nairobi Readers to come, to celebrate the wedding.

There have been many narrations of what happened on October 7th[1], 2000 at the Wedding of Opposites. The following pages are therefore more a collage of various insights than a narration. Some Readers have said these sixteen readings could be the beginning of The October Book (I myself wonder if *Two Readers* itself might become the October Book). In any case Part Four should be read less as narration and more as meditation.

---

[1] October 7th is the Feast of The Holy Rosary (in Nairobi, after the wedding, we now spell it: Whole–y Rosary). The month of October is known in the Catholic world as "The month of the Rosary."

These readings first appeared in *The Special Millennial Edition of Wasomaji* published in October 2001 (a year after the wedding). Interspersed in the events of the Wedding Day are Sixteen Readings: eight were read at the grave and eight at the reception.

The Grave Setting and some Clowning Around

Liberita, Special Millenial Edition of the Wasomaji, October, 2001

The grave of Lwanga was in the eastern corner of the Nairobi arboretum where on this October day the rising sun was splashing light on the purple flowers of a Jacaranda tree in full bloom. I was sitting on a purple-petaled, white marble-bench at the foot of the Ibisaji's grave taking in the scents of the trees around me. My nose in that morning world was reading an alphabet of aromas quite different from the hideous stink of Kikomba where I had grown up. I suddenly felt a deep gratitude toward the man buried beneath these trees. Though I had never met Lwanga I had benefited from all that he had taught Rama and Agio. I had him to thank for the fact that I could afford a flat at the edge of this tree park where I supported my siblings by teaching literacy at a nearby primary school. I had him plus Naibis to thank for the volunteer job I held now at the Wasomaji newspaper. Being its editor had challenged me to grow as both a reader and a writer. The thought of her made me look at the grave next to Lwanga's, the place where his Ibis was buried. Many people, as I remember it, expected Naibis to disappear forever when the Ibis died (murdered by a book-hater). But she surprised them when she reappeared a few weeks later quite her normal self except for an uncanny fear of dictionaries.

My reason for coming early to the gravesite was to pray with Naibis before the Redbeads and Greenbeads arrived. She had suggested we could read the joyful and sorrowful mysteries at seven a.m before the others came to read the glorious at eight a.m. Tt was now seven thirty, where was she? Just then I heard a clucking noise and she suddenly appeared from behind the headstone of the Ibis. Naibis opened the rainbow shawl she had around her shoulders and with her strong arms she embraced me. She sheltered me in those warm shawl-wings and held me for a full two minutes and then said, or rather chuckled, "I am late, we don't have time for the unabridged rosary so lets do the abridged version." That was fine with me so we sat down on the bench, hand in hand, and started the Bead-Game.[2] "I spy the color red," she intoned. I looked around and pointed to the Utopian Eucalyptus at the right side of Lwanga's grave, and said, "Uzazi Zeal!"

Now it was my turn. "I spy the color green," I intoned. She looked around and pointed to the lovely Thevetia at the left side of Lwanga's grave, and said "*Urembo wa Ulimwengo*."

When we had finished the Bead-Game of five red riddles and five green riddles the guests began to arrive. Perhaps they wondered why we would be laughing at the side of a grave but they did not say anything. A moment later Rama and Agio walked up to the grave of their Reading Guide and then the ceremony began.

I had the First Two Readings so I stood up from the bench. Naibis gave me a wink and an encouraging smile.

THE FIRST READING
How was Lwanga Wounded?

Liberita, Special Millennial Edition of the Wasomaji, October 2001

How did Lwanga get wounded? Agio and Rama omitted that detail when telling the story of his last days. The fact is Lwanga died from a bullet wound.

It was a sort of accident. Though Lwanga seldom got visitors

---

[2] She took the name from *Magister Ludi* a book about beads that had won Herman Hesse the Nobel Peace prize for literature.

while he was in prison, he did get a visit each day from his Ibis.

One day the Ibis was landing on the prison courtyard where Lwanga stood waving. A prison guard who was drunk was observing the bird. The man was only five feet from Lwanga and he could smell the alcohol on the man's breath.

When the Ibis landed, the guard lifted his rifle to shoot it. Lwanga quickly pushed the gun barrel down. By so doing he made the gun go off – into his thigh.

After two weeks in the prison hospital, unattended, Lwanga became feverish. His wound was septic. Remember, too, he had already come down with pneumonia from the cold, wet cell, and was weak, even before he got wounded.

Rama, alarmed, got permission and took Lwanga home. The wounded Leader of Readers was placed on his bed in his flat at the rear of the bookstore. He suffered there for a week and three days. Mind you, he was still a prisoner. In fact, once when the probation officer was coming to visit, Rama had to handcuff Lwanga to the bed.

Let me not forget Agio. He too visited his reading teacher. Often, in fact. But Rama would always leave the flat whenever Agio entered it. They never spoke a word to each other as one went in and the other went out.

Lwanga was dead and buried several years before Agio made the famous phone call to Rama that was the beginning of the reconciliation and reunion this book is all about.

THE SECOND READING
A New Eve: Lwanga's Song

Lwanga

> I am the voice
> of the twenty first century,
> of those weary of tribal hate
> and the wars of the last century.

> My voice not tribal African
> but Genesis African,
> living in Nairobi
> near the empty tomb of Eve.

> I am the voice
> of the new unity,
> of the rainbow continent,
> of mingled bloods and colors.

> My voice not tribal African
> but Genesis African,
> living in Nairobi
> near the empty tomb of Eve.

> I sing to give heart,
> liver, brains, guts,
> – maternal zeal –
> to you, Glorious Generation.

> Through you I will vanquish ethnic hate.
> Through you I will vanquish hunger.
> Through you I will vanquish illness.
> Through you I will put things right for children.

> My voice not tribal African

but Genesis African,
living in Nairobi
near the empty tomb of Eve.

Found in Lwanga's pocket the day he was shot, protecting the Ibis.

What Happened Next at the Wedding of Opposites

Liberita

After the first two readings I sat down.

Agio and Rama stood up at the foot of Lwanga's grave and stared at it for a full five minutes. With tears in his eyes, Rama took penciled paper from his pocket and read an apology to Ibis. Then Agio and Rama read a joint confession to Ibis and to their fellow Readers. They turned to each other and embraced. After the embrace they read a poem that they had co-written. You have thus the third, fourth and fifth readings.

Then everyone turned and faced the words written on the gravestones of Lwanga and his Ibis. Agio read that of Ibisaji and Rama that of Ibis. You have thus the sixth and seventh readings.

Finally the Reader leaders shared with us what they called The Doctrine of Enantiodromia: a new teaching about Lectio. This is the eighth reading.

THE THIRD READING
Forgive Me Ibis!

Rama, Special Millennial Edition of Wasomaji, October 2001

Why did I slay beauty
    with a dictionary?
Why did I kill Ibis?

Because I was afraid of reading:
Changing the world was scary,
Accepting it was more so…

Because I refused to be affected
Receptive, open, porous,
I killed the Albatross …

Because I wanted control not coleridge,
And could not simply sit and enjoy leisure
I killed the reading spirit…

Because I was afraid of the secret knowledge,
The God-awful wings, the freedom
You wanted to give me, Readers' Guide!

THE FOURTH READING
Ibis Forgive Us

Co-Written by Rama and Agio, Special Millennial Edition of the Wasomaji, October 2001

We wanted to confess. We wanted to confess for years. We were unable. Do you know why?

We were unable because we were perfect. We were had never failed. What had we to confess?

Perfect—perfect book-termites. We bore into pages and never left the page. We never fell because we never tried to fly. We didn't want wings. We preferred crawling between book covers. We were book-termites without wings. We feared lectio.

Now we understand. Perfection does not have wings. To read, to fly, well, it means to embrace the scary other, the stranger-me, the me-not-in-control, the me liable to make mistakes, the imperfect me.

Once we embraced the other in ourselves we got wings. Even if they're not Ibis wings, only termite wings, still we can fly.

Now we understand. Propagandists are perfect. Poets never are.

A haunted person is not harrowed by a strange presence but by a strange absence.

Each of us was haunted by a *life-not-being-lived* (a phantom life).

Each edited himself, each preferred to be a caricature of his stronger side: a living hagiography.

Now it is clear. We were two haunted men. Each haunted by the holes, the lacunae, the missing imperfection in our vaunted hagiographies.

But look—what is hagiography? Is it not biography that's been expurgated?

If you edify yourself:
You expurgate what is opposite,
You take out the wild unknown,
You *denature holiness* and, then; See,
You've destroyed the very thing you were seeking to create-
Without your imperfections you can't be a saint.

Rilke defined haunted as a sense that something is missing.
The sense that people have of impermanence
and perishing comes mostly from their own
not-having-been-ness.
In order to be,
it is not enough to be born.

THE FIFTH READING
The Embrace

Co-written by Agio and Rama, Special Millennial Edition of the
Wasomaji, October 2001

> Sleeping in the arbor
> On fallen peepul leaves
> I dreamed Ngugi wa Thiongo[3]
> Was dancing with Okot B'Bitek.[4]
>
> Red and Green in me embracing.
>
> Before waking
> On fallen peepul leaves
> I dreamed Lord Quixote
> Was dancing with Squire Sancho.
> Was dancing with Squire Sancho.
>
> Red and Green in me embracing.
>
> Sitting up on the peepul leaves I laughed
> At the odd picnickers now in the arbor:
> Al Camus and Oscar Wilde,
> Al Schweitzer and Joy Adamson.
>
> Red and Green in me embracing.

---

[3] *Ngugi wa Thiongo* –A Kenyan writer whose main theme is social justice.
[4] *Okot B'Bitek* –A Kenyan writer whose main theme is beauty and joyful song.

Ibis

THE SIXTH AND SEVENTH READINGS
Texts of the Two Tombstones

IBISAJI
A BOOK LOVER

When you come to the edge of all the light that you know you will be given wings ...

LWANGA
1937-1992
NAIROBI

The Founder of The Circle Readers

IBIS
A BOOK LOVER

And when the Dragon saw that he had been thrown to the earth, he pursued the woman who had borne the child. But the woman was given the two wings of the great eagle that she might fly from the serpent ...

LWANGA
1963-1999
NAIROBI

The Reading Spirit Which Never Dies

THE EIGHTH READING
The Doctrine of Enantiodromia

Co-written by Rama and Agio, Special Millennial Edition of the Wasomaji, October 2001

Question: What is the purpose of lectio?

Answer: To journey with R. G. Marie through the mysteries of joy and the mysteries of sorrow until you reach the point where you can participate with joy in the sorrows of the world.[5] Then you start to live a glorious life. You are engaged, burning, exuberant. Finally you've become a word in context.

This is what the Word of God did. Readers have always considered the Incarnation as a divine contextualization: the *Great I AM* put in context. How else could God be readable?

To be readable one must be in context: green needs a red background; red needs a green background.

Rama contextualizes Agio.

Agio contextualizes Rama.

Read out of context, joy is silly.

Read out of context, sorrow is morose.

The purpose of lectio is to reach the point where one participates with *joy* in the *sorrows* of the world, the point where finally one is useful.

Rabindranath Tagore, an artist who fought for justice in India, wrote:

> "I slept and dreamt that life was joy
> I woke and saw that life was service
> I acted and behold! Service was joy."

---

[5] To participate with joy in the sorrows of the world is a phrase coined by Joseph Campbell to describe the glorious life (which he called Bliss).

Lwanga's Last Wish: Reading the Mysteries of Bliss

Liberita Special Millennial Edition of the Wasomaji, October 2001.

Rama and Agio then invited the twelve and I to stand in a circle around the grave of Lwanga and pray with them the Glorious Mysteries, which are each a punchline to jokes we had feared were not jokes but "the hard facts of life:" – failure – exile – fear – humiliation – incompleteness.

The funniest thing happens:
Resurrection: Failure Embraces Forgiveness
Ascension: The Paradox of Leaving Home to come Home
Pentecost: Fear Embraces Faith
Assumption: The Paradox of the Lowly Raised up.
Coronation: The End (Eve Two) embraces the Beginning (Eve One) The human project is completed , comes full circle.

While the Readers were reciting the last decade of this rosary tears came to my eyes. I walked behind the headstones and put a hand on each one. After the readers had put away their rosaries I said, "At the end of his confession Rama wrote about a glimpse of future glory he had when a child died at Kenyatta Hospital.

"It might seem odd that the two readers – opposites in everything else – would enter the Mysteries of Glory in the same way. But it is not odd to anyone who has seen a child die. At that point one must decide either for a universe in which such happens period or a universe in which such happens comma. Rama and Agio both decided to look at it as the wise old woman (Gracie Allen) who said: "Never put a period where God has placed a comma." Both the Risen Lord and the Assumpta would agree.

"This is what we Living owe the Dead: to imagine them in glory. This is the purpose of the Glorious Mysteries. The innocent dead—if we imagine them in glory—do not then become Martyrs for the Devil. The Seducer of the whole world, that red dragon of the Book of Revelation, does not then devour the child, does not make the child a martyr for the devil, that Hopeless Cynic. Their deaths do not make us give up our faith in the struggle. Imagining the emaciated child who died of hunger or HIV-tainted blood, alive, above us in heaven (or ahead of us in the New Millennium), suckled by the full breasted Assumpta who sings "The hungry will be given good things to eat," imagining a future beyond failure, and futility, this is what it means to read the last five mysteries of the rosary."

I kissed the headstones and walked back to where I had been standing. Naibis winked at me. She too was crying, but also, at the same time, laughing.

Two Readers Remain at the Graveside of Readers' Guide.

After this the six Redbeads made a solemn bow to the headstones and turning toward Rama bowed again. They slowly walked out of the arboretum with their heads lowered. The six Greenbeads then each blew a kiss toward the headstones and turning toward Agio did the same beaugeste again. Their exit from the arboretum was just as slow as the Redbeads but their green-filled heads were not hanging quite as low.

Rama, Agio, Naibis and I watched the Redbeads and Greenbeads walk down the hill toward the old bookstore making their way in two separate processions. Knowing that I would have to run ahead and open the bookstore I broke the silence and said,

"Have to carry on......"
     "You'll need two arms." Naibis said.
"Must be running......"
     "You'll need two legs." Naibis said.
"Well I'll see you......"
     "With two eyes." Naibis said.

Perplexed by Naibis and this irreverent bye bye banter the

Two Readers put their arms akimbo and shook their heads at her. Naibis sat down on a bench at the foot of the grave and said, "Come sit at either side of me; I want to ask you something." Rama and Agio let their indignation pass and took their hands from their hips. The doctor sat down at the left side of the old lady, the painter at her right.

"Have you ever read the plays of Ibsen?" Naibis asked.

"Yes he was a great artist," Agio said.

"I've also read him. His main theme was social justice," Rama said.

"What do you think his last words were?" inquired Naibis.

"A summary of his beliefs," replied Agio.

"He clarified his position, most likely," replied Rama,, "and gave a final, full, and firm expression of his life's work."

Naibis shook her head and raised her eyebrows, " 'On the other hand,' those were his last words. That's what he said to the Ibsen Readers gathered around him waiting for his definitive last words. 'On the other hand,' that was his final position."

Agio looked at the green leaves of the trees. Rama stared at the headstones.

Naibis continued, "The irony of it." She bent over and picked up a leaf from the ground. "When chlorophyll retreats from the leaf it turns red." Then she pointed to the graves, 'When blood retreats from the body it turns green." She horrified the Two Readers by laughing. "In the end everything becomes its opposite."

Agio and Rama turned toward the birdish lady who sat between them. She pulled in her legs and swiveled around on the bench. She put her left hand on Agio's head and her right hand on Rama's head. She chuckled and said, "R.G. Marie has sometimes been called 'Our Lady of the Last Laugh.' Her song has laughter in it as if she can see the opposite of everything: the poor made rich, the hungry well fed. An English Prime Minister was known as the Iron Lady. I think, for us, R.G. Marie is the Lady of Irony."

Naibis still facing the opposite direction, took from her pockets two envelopes. "Here," she said. "Lectio the contents of these envelopes. Before he died Lwanga gave them to me and said I should give them to you on the day you come to his grave and pray together. Stay here a while. There's no rush. I'll join Liberita at the Bookstore. We'll prepare a sip of coffee for you and the others who just left. It will be something very small but do pass by on your way home." Naibis started down the hill looking up at the trees of the arboretum. She paused for a moment under the Cypress, cackled and walked on toward the bookstore.

The Two Readers alone by themselves opened their envelopes and lectio-ed the contents: a red heart for Rama, a green heart for Agio, and these notes attached.

> *Dear Rama,*
>
> *If you had a better sense of irony you could see how funny you are and laugh at yourself.*
> *When you reunited with Agio the Joy-Bird laid a dark egg in the center of your red heart; gaze a minute on it what do you see?*
>
> *Yours in Enantiodromia,*
> *Lwanga.*

> *Dear Agio,*
>
> *If you had a better sense of irony you could see how funny you are and laugh at yourself.*
> *When you reunited with Rama the Sorrow-Bird laid a dark egg in the center of your green heart; gaze a minute on it what do you see?*
>
> *Yours in Enantiodromia,*
> *Lwanga.*

The Two Readers did as they were asked. After this they found a message written on the inside flap of their respective envelopes. It said;

Rainbow Beatitude

Blessed are you who laugh at the sight
of your many selves in the glass at night.
You will picnic in the fields of light.

The Reception We Gave Two Readers at the Resurrected Bookstore

Liberita, Special Millennial Edition of the Wasomaji, October, 2001.

"Surprise!" shouted Naibis as Rama and Agio walked into the old bookstore. Lights went on and green and red confetti showered the two readers. Readers were throwing confetti and singing ReUnited, a disco song popular when Rama and Agio were young men. Naibis and I, along with the twelve Readers at the wedding ceremony had variously begged, cajoled, and threatened the Nairobi Readers to come to a "wedding reception" in honor of Rama and Agio following their joint confessions at Lwanga's grave. And the Readers came – there were almost a hundred people on the ground floor of Readers' Guide!

Rama held Agio's hand and smiled. Agio pointed to the green and red bunting hanging from the rafters. Rama pointed to the red and green streamers looped on the face of the bookshelves that were no longer empty.

I escorted the two Readers to the drumtable in the chat corner where they were served with buttered hot scones and freshly brewed Arabica Coffee.

"Please be seated," I said.

Then all the Redbeads and Greenbeads sat down in chairs that were arranged in a circle around two statues in the middle of the room.

I was the Master of Ceremonies. Once all the Redbeads and Greenbeads were seated, and while Rama and Agio were sipping their coffee, I introduced myself and the Resurrected Bookstore.

"For those who do not know me, my name is Liberita. I am the editor of the *Wasomaji, which*, as you know, is a community newspaper, your newspaper, the common property of the Nairobi Circle of Readers. As you also know, the *Wasomaji* was about to close down because of the boycott of the Redbeads and Greenbeads." I stopped and looked around the circle at each of the seated Readers. "But, based on the number of Redbeads and Greenbeads present here today, I would venture to say that the boycott is over."

"The boycott is over," shouted a Redbead. A Greenbead shouted the same words, "The boycott is over." Then the room became quiet, very quiet, and, suddenly the whole Circle of Readers broke into applause.

The applause continued for a full five minutes. I sat down and tried to take in the wonderful scene before me. The Circle of Readers was seated around a life-size statue of the Pieta and a life-size statue of the Madonna.

(The red marble statue of the Pieta, which usually holds the slain body of the crucified Jesus, had an empty lap. The green statue of the Madonna, which usually holds the baby Jesus, also had an empty lap.)

A hundred candles – red and green – had been stuck in a pile of loose arboretum soil. The candles were burning in honor of the Pieta and the Madonna. It was a wonderful scene indeed. But I noticed that Rama and Agio were staring more at the soil than at the candles. Perhaps it reminded them of their youthful encounters with the Ibis.

When the applause stopped I stood up and said, "We have come here today to celebrate the reunion of Redbeads and Greenbeads and to reopen Readers' Guide." More applause!

"Thank you friends, this is a happy day, a day the Lord has made, let us be glad and rejoice." People were stomping their feet and applauding at the same time. When it quieted down I said, "In our program today we will play and pray. Let the first half of our time together be a playful wedding of bodies: lift your glasses, dance to the music. Let the second half of our time together be a prayerful wedding of souls: lift your beads, lectio to the mixed texts."

I winked at Naibis who was standing behind Rama and Agio. She walked to the circle and through it up to the statue of the Pieta. She bent down to a prayer mat in front of the statue (Lwanga's red ibis rug) and lifted a pile of papers from it. She gave one of the papers to each of the Redbeads and said, "You are devoted to the red Heart of Mary. And your love is fearless. So stare long and hard into the center of this red heart. What do you see?" After a few minutes Naibis said, "When you stare long enough at death what you see my Redbead friends is life! Love is fearless. Be not afraid of death. *Be not afraid of life!*"

Naibis then walked up to the statue of the Madonna. She bent down to a prayer mat in front of the statue (Lwanga's green ibis rug) and lifted a pile of papers from it. She gave one of the papers to each of the Greenbeads and said, "You are devoted to the green Heart of Mary. And your love is fearless. So stare long and hard into the center of this green heart. What do you see?" After a few minutes Naibis said, "When you stare long enough at life what you see my friends is death! Love is fearless. Be not afraid of life. *Be not afraid of death.*"

Naibis went back to the chat corner and stood behind Rama and Agio. Then I said, "Strange as it may sound, those were party favors. The next thing that happens at a wedding reception is a round of toasts. Let me begin." I raised my glass and said:

"To Blood and Chlorophyll;

To Rama and Agio!"

Then I sat down, looked around the room, and said, "Please, let's have more toasts!" The Readers responded to my request with enthusiasm. Here's what followed:

"To the Kenyan Flag;
To Ngugi Wa Thiongo and Okot B. Bitek!"

"To the Italian Flag;
To Garibaldi and Fellini!"

"To Sunrise through Pine Trees;
To Edel Quinn and Karen Blixen!"

"To the Robes of Consolata;
To Zorba and Zoro!"

"To the Bougainvillea;
To Doctor Schweitzer and Doctor Seuss!"

"To Neapolitan Ice Cream;
To Quixote and Sancho!"

"To the Poinsettia;
To Jomo Kenyatta and Bill Cosby!"

"To our candles here;
To the Evangelists Mark and Luke!"

"And, finally, to the Chameleon;
To R. G. Marie: Pieta and Madonna!"

After the toasts and a few glasses of wine the assembly was
quite animated. When the music began Agio and Rama stood up,
clapped their hands and shook their bodies. Then Redbeads and
Greenbeads turned to each other and asked for a dance. Ahh. The
day had come. If only Lwanga had lived to see this day.

Naibis sang a song in honor of Lwanga.

THE NINETH READING
Color Radio Dancing

by Naibis

> Life is dancing,
> Dancing a circle.
>
> Two readers dance:
> to recharge each other,
> to evoke each other,
> out of themselves again.
>
> The D.J. says, "*I piped you*
> life green and red,
> But you would not dance
> to its joy and sorrow."
>
> So their life is at a standstill
> the colors have stopped dancing.
>
> Hey, Agio and Rama
> time to tune in.
> Switch your stations
> to Color Radio!
>
> Jesus, the D.J. of rainbow waves,
> and the Lord of Circles,
> Pipes you life green and red.
> dance to the music of colors .

After about an hour of dancing Naibis signaled to the Disc Jockey and the music stopped. I stood up and said, "The first half of our time together is over and now we want to begin the wedding of souls and the lectio of mixed texts."

Naibis walked to the center of the circle as I signaled to the

Readers to sit down. Naibis spoke. "Friends," she said, "I have asked Liberita to lead us in the recitation of the rosary. Rama and Agio have agreed that Liberita should from this day on lead the Circle of Readers in the recitation of the rosary here at Readers' Guide every Saturday. We would like to resume our communal lectio. Whoever is in favor please raise your hand." Almost immediately hands shot into the air. But what amazed me most is that everyone in the room was in favor of the proposal. All hands were raised. Sighing, Naibis turned around in the middle of the Circle of Readers, and said, "Thank you." Then she sat down and nodded at me.

"To begin, let me greet you in the name of the Readers' Guide, R. G. Marie. I welcome you in the name of Our Lady of Enantiodromia to this recitation of the Joyful and Sorrowful and Glorious Mysteries."

We all made the sign of the cross and then I said, "Since this is October 7th 2000, the first feast of the Most Holy Rosary in the new millennium, I am going to lead us in what I call the Jubilee Rosary."

Rama and Agio were back in the chat corner seated around the drumtable. I turned to them and said, "Would you please stand up and tell us the five greatest sorrows of the last thousand years and the five greatest joys of the last thousand years."

Rama got to his feet and, almost breathless, unable to chronologize in his haste, he began a litany of woes:

The AIDS Epidemic
The Slave Trade
The Legalization of Abortion
The Crusades, Wars of Religion, and All Wars
Famines in Biafra, in the Sahel, in the Sudan,
    in Ethiopia, and in Somalia

"These, my fellow Red... I mean, these, dear Readers, are the sorrows I used to discuss at this very table with Lwanga. This gallant store reminds me so much of the Ibisaji and his full commitment to the Red Vocation."

When Rama sat down Agio got to his feet. He also was frantic in his own way. He also did not have the presence of mind to chronologize. He said:

Lady Joy's *Portraits of Kenyans*
Cézanne's *Water Lilies*
Michelangelo's *Creation of Adam*
Van Gogh's *Sunflowers*
Fra Angelica's *Annunciation*

"My fellow Green... I mean, dear Readers, these are the joys I used to talk over with Lwanga at this very table. This beautiful old bookstore reminds me so much of the Ibis Keeper and his complete commitment to the Green Vocation."

When Agio sat down I said, "Rama and Agio, each of you talks as if you only knew one side of Lwanga. Let me refresh your memory. In the Journals you donated to the *Wasomaji* I came across these gems."

A Redbead stood up and read from Rama's Journal:

THE TENTH READING
A Memory of Lwanga and the Children

by Rama, 3 June[6], 1985

One day on the ground floor of the Readers' Guide Bookstore I found Lwanga getting a painting lesson from a group of street children.

Twenty of them had just finished eating the daily milk and bread Lwanga provided every morning.

---

[6] 3rd June is the Feast Day of St. Charles Lwanga, and in 1985 it was the Centenary of his martyrdom.

The satisfied eaters were about to go out the door and back to their daily grind.

It is then that Lwanga suddenly surprised the children by asking if they would stay a while because he wanted their advice.

I recorded the remarkable exchange I heard that morning. I've tried to put it into meter.

"What Color Joy?"

"Tell me child of two, what color shall I use
to paint the Annunciation?"

"White of the glad flowers of the morning glory,"
replied the boy as he fled away with giggle and glee.

"Tell me child of four, what color shall I pour
to paint the Visitation?"

"Blue of the bell flowers of the blue plumbago,"
replied the girl as she put in her hair a ribbon bow.

"Tell me child of six, what color shall I mix
to paint the Nativity?"

"Green red of the star flowers and of the green red poinsettia" replied the boy as he ate biscuits at the kitchen *meza*.

"Tell me child of eight, what color shall I take
to paint the Presentation?"

"Orange of the wing feathers of the bird of

paradise," replied the girl as she jumped rope, once, twice, thrice.

"Tell me child of ten what colors shall I blend to paint the Temple Finding?"

"Egg-white pink of the hoof flowers on the camel feet tree," replied the boy as he handed my paints and brush to me.

When the Redbead finished reading from Rama's Journal he sat down. Then a Greenbead stood up and read from Agio's journal:

THE ELEVENTH READING
A Memory of Lwanga and the Children

By Agio, 3 June, 1991[7]

I'm standing as I write this. I am standing behind the counter of Readers' Guide filling in for Lwanga. He is in the classroom, teaching his weekly class of street children.

I can hear them repeat after him:

"A ni kwa Arusi.
B ni kwa Bata
C ni kwa Cool
D ni kwa Daraja
E ni kwa Elimu"

---

[7] The 106th anniversary of St. Charles Lwanga's death and the birthday of the *Watoto wa Lwanga* (children of Lwanga) project which gives street children in Nairobi the world of reading and writing.

Lwanga does not pretend to accomplish much in his hour a week. But he promised himself long ago to tutor the child whose education he sponsors. This year he is paying for five children at the St. Peter Claver Primary School. And all of them are in the cellar right now, singing:

"You are my sunshine,
My only sunshine...

"You'll never know dear,
How much I love you..."

He likes to teach children that song. And he has them slap their knees and clap to it.

Oh yes, now I hear him talking about the drums. This is always the November lesson.

He is reading Whitman to them. Just like he read him to me...

"Beat! beat! drums! – blow! bugles! blow!
Through windows – through doors –
burst like a ruthless force
Into the solemn church and scatter the congregation
Into the school where the scholar is studying."

I can't hear what he is saying now. He is probably speaking in a low serious voice. But I can guess what he is saying. He's telling the children, as he told me, "You are *Iregi*.[8] You are brave fighters. In Europe they were called Knights. Here in Africa they are called *Iregi*. The drums call you. The voices of the ancestors call you to stand up and fight for what is right. If you see someone smaller than you unable to defend herself you must stand up and fight for that child. Now listen to me and I'll tell you the story of the *Iregi*..."

Still at the counter, I think about the twelve-year-old boy on the front bench who is listening to Lwanga. I imagine his eyes going big when Lwanga says the phrase, "African Chivalry." The drum beckons the boy into bliss, "Giving your life is life-giving! The *Iregi* gave themselves to something greater than themselves. That has always been and will always be the secret to happiness." And then to end, Lwanga beats Mandela's drumtaps to them: "*Nzoki Sikelele* Africa."[9]

When the Greenbead finished reading from Agio's Journal he sat down. Then I stood up and said to Rama and Agio, "Have you

---

[8] *Iregi* – The generation of warriors who stood by the oppressed.
[9] *Nzoki Sikelele Africa* - The Liberation Song used during the struggle against Apartheid; it is now South Africa's National Anthem.

anything to say?"

They were sitting by the drumtable that had scone crumbs on it, and empty cups of coffee and empty glasses of wine. They looked at each other very serious, full of intensity, and, suddenly, broke out laughing. Rama spoke first. "I am sorry that I deliberately closed myself to Lwanga's green side. Indeed, I was aware of it, but I would not let him teach me anything about joy."

Agio spoke next. "I am also sorry that I deliberately closed myself to Lwanga's red side. Indeed, I was aware of it, but would not let him teach me anything about sorrow."

Naibis had been standing behind the two Readers. When they were asking to be forgiven she walked in front of them. When they finished their speeches she looked long and hard into their eyes and said, "You're both forgiven."

Then Naibis opened her arms to the two Readers and said, "Let's move it." She laughed and bent over and lifted the drumtable and carried it, half dragging it, to the center of the Circle of Readers, directly in front of the red and green statues. Rama and Agio tried to clear the cups and glasses off the table as it was being transported but things were falling off all over the floor. It didn't bother Naibis. She laughed and said, "I couldn't wait a minute longer to get you over to R. G. Marie."

Once the drumtable and chairs had been rearranged in the middle of the room and Rama and Agio were seated there, Naibis said, "Have you anything to say to the Redbeads and Greenbeads who turned down the invitation to the reunion reception today?"

Agio stood up first. He pulled a crumpled, soiled paper out of his pocket. He hardly had to look down at it. He knew it by heart. He must have been reciting this message to any Greenbead who would listen.

THE TWELFTH READING
Where There's Smolder There's Ashes

By Agio

Strolling past my window
tourists, day-trippers,
lie-abouts, and leisurists,
You Nairobians.

Green the color of corpses, you put the fire out.

Strolling past my window
to game parks, to film shows,
to arbors, and sweet reverie,
You Nairobians.

Green the color of corpses, you put the fire out.

Strolling past my window
away from the sight of hunger,
away from the voices crying,
You Nairobians.

Green the color of corpses, you put the fire out.

Strolling past my window
thinking nothing can be done,
thinking everything has been tried,
You Nairobians.

Green the color of corpses, you put the fire out.

Strolling past my window
away from the rage you fear,
away from an indignation that would save you,

Nairobians.

Green the color of corpses, you put the fire out.

After Agio finished appealing to the Greenbeads who had refused the invitation to Readers' Guide he sat down. Then Rama stood up, pulled a crumpled, soiled paper out of his pocket. He also did not need to look down at it. He must have recited it hundreds of times. Here is what he said.

THE THIRTEENTH READING
Slow-Fire or What's the Rush?

by Rama

> Rushing past my window
> clerks, typists, storekeepers,
> drivers, sweepers, cooks,
> You Nairobians.
>
> *Red burns too fast.*
> Be green and red instead.
>
> Rushing past my window
> to count, to write, to sell,
> to travel, to clean, to bake,
> You Nairobians.
>
> *Red burns too fast.*
> Be green and red instead.
>
> Rushing past my window
> You're so serious;
> Do you know
> Without humor nothing is serious.

Red burns too fast.
Be green and red instead.

Rushing past my window
sing a song, laugh out loud,
mingle your labor with leisure.
You are more than what you do.

Red burns too fast.
Be green and red instead.

You need not
rush past my window.
See that green bench,
it's there for you, *karibu*.

Red burns too fast.
Be green and red instead.

Don't rush to your next task, give it worth;
sit on my green bench and finger your red beads,
then you'll do great things with rainbow ease.
With joy participate in the sorrows of the earth.

Red burns too fast.
Be green and red instead;
    A Fire Glorious;
    Slow, but enormous.

    When Agio and Rama had finished their appeals I stood up and looked around the room. "These two Readers, our leaders, failed to listen to each other an hour ago when I asked them to name the great joys and sorrows of the last thousand years. Now I ask the Jubilee question to all of you. But, please turn to the person you are sitting next to and listen to their five joys. Let them share:

"One personal joy, the most beautiful thing that's ever happened to them;

"Two national joys, the two most beautiful things ever to happen in Kenya;

"Two global joys, the two most beautiful things ever to happen in the world."

After a period of quiet discussion, one to one, that lasted about ten minutes I said, "Let's see how well you listened. Would anyone like to share a national joy or a global joy you heard from your neighbor?" A few people volunteered to speak. Here is a random sampling of what they said:

Ten great joys for Kenya according to the Circle of Readers are:

The Arrival of the Gospel, *Ukweli*[10]!
The Departure of the British, *Uhuru*!
The UNICEF Vaccination Program
The Democracy Movement Creates a Multi-Party Kenya
Holy Ghost Priests Plant the First Coffee Bush in Kenya
Kenya Achieves One of the Highest Literacy Rates in Africa
Readers' Guide Bookstore Opens
Martyr's Bloodbank Opens
The Wasomaji Newspaper is First Published
Kenya runners win Olympic Medals

Ten great joys for the World according to the Circle of Readers are:

The Discovery of the African Origins of the Human Race
Abraham Lincoln Issuing the Emancipation Proclamation
The Invention of the Record Player
The signing of the French "*Droits des Hommes*"
New Zealand is the 1st Nation to Give Women the Vote

---

[10] Truth.

The End of Apartheid in South Africa
The Technical Capacity to End World Hunger
The Invention of the Light Bulb
The Papal Proclamation of the Assumption
The Invention of the Printing Press

"Keep these joys in mind," I said, "as we pray the joyful decades of the rosary. I would like us to use the following Hail Mary for the joyful mysteries we are meditating on.

"Hail Green Mary,
Full of Joy,
The Lord is with you.

"Blessed are you among artists,
And blessed your creative exuberance,
Jesus the Word.

"Holy Madonna,
Mother of God,
Pray for us Readers
Now and at the *Kairos*
Of Extreme Pleasure.
Amen."

While we were reciting this Green Ave Naibis was giving a green colored egg to each of the Readers. She bent over close to their ears and whispered, "Exuberance."

After each decade we did a choral refrain. I would stop and say, "What is Capax Dei?" The Readers responded, "To Participate with Joy in the Sorrows of the World."

After the recitation of the Joyful Mysteries I said, "Let us now reflect on the sorrows of the last thousand years. Please turn to the person you are sitting next to and listen to the five sorrows they select as the greatest:

One personal sorrow, the most painful thing that has ever

happened to them;

Two national sorrows, the most painful two that have happened in Kenya;

Two global sorrows, the most painful two that have happened in the world."

After a ten-minute period of quiet one-to-one discussion I said, "Let's see how well you listened. Would anyone like to share a national sorrow or a global sorrow you heard from your neighbor?" A few people volunteered to speak. Here is a random sampling of what they said:

Ten great sorrows for Kenya according to the Circle of Readers are:

Colonialism, Racism, Tribalism, Sexism
AIDS
The Bombing of the American Embassy
Famine Every Ten Years
Malaria, Cholera, and Other Water Borne Diseases
Increasing Rates of Abortion
The Increasing Number of Street children
The Death of Lwanga and the Closing of his Bookstore
The Schism in the Circle of Readers
The Bankruptcy of Martyrs' Bloodbank

Ten great sorrows for the World according to the Circle of Readers are:

Colonialism, Racism, Sexism
AIDS
World Hunger
World Wars
Genocide committed against Jews, Armenians, and Tutsis
Water Borne Diseases
Increasing Rates of Abortion
The Increasing Number of Street children
The widening gap between rich countries and poor countries

The Bombing of New York and Washington[11]

"Keep these sorrows in mind," I said as we pray the sorrowful mysteries of the rosary. I would like us to use the following Hail Mary as we meditate on the sorrows that have been mentioned:

"Hail Red Mary,
Full of Sorrow,
The Lord is with you.

"Blessed are you among activists,
And blessed your fiery exuberance,
Jesus the Word.

"Holy Pieta,
Mother of Red Mysteries,
Pray for us Readers,
Now and at the *Kairos*
Of Extreme Pain.
Amen."

While we were reciting this Red Ave Naibis was giving a red colored egg to each of the Readers. She bent over close to their ears and whispered, "Exuberance."

After each decade we did a choral refrain. I would stop and say, "What is '*Capax Dei*?'" The Readers responded, "To Participate with Joy in the Sorrows of the World."

Once we had finished the Sorrowful Mysteries I said, "We have come to a very important moment in the Jubilee Rosary. We must pause here before we enter the Glorious Mysteries. I have asked Naibis to reflect on the joys and sorrows of these past fifty

---

[11] This had not yet happened in October 2000 but Naibis and I added it in the Special Millennial Edition published in October 2001 (a month after the bombing) because this act of terrorism deeply affected Nairobians since we were bombed in a similar way in 1998.

years; that is, the joys and sorrows of The Two Readers. What she is about to say will help us all because we've all been caught up in the extremities and drama of these two lives. And so sit back a while. This will take a few minutes. We've come midway in our liturgy; the "How-Can-This-Be Homily."

Naibis entered the circle and stood by Rama and Agio, by Pieta and Madonna. She read:

THE FOURTEENTH READING
How-Can-This-Be Homily

> The first thing R. G. Marie says in the Gospel is "How can this be?" The first thing out of the young woman's mouth is a question; it's the same question Rama and Agio try to answer as young men: "How can this be?"
>
> The young doctor looks around at all the suffering in the world and asks, "How can *this* be? This much sorrow, *this* great suffering." And then the right books appear (the Word) from the book supplier. The world (which was created by the Word) becomes readable.
>
> The young painter looks around at all the heartbreaking beauty in the world and asks, "How can *this* be? This much joy, *this* great beauty." And then the right books appear (the Word) from the book supplier. The world (which was created by the Word) becomes readable.
>
> Do you see? R. G. Marie gave young Rama the books that contained the Word

in blood. She gave young Agio the books that contained the Word in bud.

There is not an answer to the question, "How can this be?," but there are a few responses. There are, in fact, as many responses as there are souls in this world. Indeed the purpose of this world of sorrow, this world of joy is to create souls. Listen to how the poet John Keats explains this world:

There may be intelligences or sparks of the divinity in millions –but they are not souls till they acquire identities, till each one is personally itself. Intelligences are atoms of perception – they know and they see and they are pure, in short they are God – how then are souls to be made? How then are these sparks which are God to have identity (contour and color) given them – so as ever to possess a bliss peculiar to each one's individual existence? How but by the medium of a world like this!_

Rama asks God, "Why do you give me this much sorrow?"

Agio asks God, "Why do you give me this much joy?"

If you listen to God as attentively as did R. G. Marie you will hear God say, "This much – no more, no less – *this is what was needed* to give you soul."

Naibis turned to Agio and Rama seated at the drumtable in front of the Green and Red statues. "Have you noticed anything unusual about these two statues?"

Rama and Agio nodded.

"What is it?" asked Naibis.

Agio said, "The Madonna has an empty lap. Where is the Green Word?"

Rama said, "The Pieta has an empty lap. Where is the Red Word?"

"I'm glad you asked," said Naibis. She left the center of the room and walked over to the staircase. She said, "Wait. I'll be right back." The Book Supplier climbed up to the next floor and then above it to the loft. We did not hear anything for a moment and then we heard her climb down from the loft to the floor below it and then to ground level. She came into the room with a big green book under one arm and a big red book under the other arm.

The Book Supplier walked into the Circle of Readers. All eyes were on her, and the books. She lifted the big green one above her head and said, "The December Book!" The assembly broke into applause. Naibis gently placed the Green Word on the lap of the Madonna.

Naibis turned to the red statue. She was now only holding the big red book. She lifted it above her head and said, "The March Book!" The whole assembly clapped their hands and stomped their feet. Naibis gently placed the Red Word on the lap of the Pieta.

Everyone thought the How-Can-This-Be Homily was finished. Then Naibis said, "Agio, go to the Pieta and pick up the March Book I've just put there." Agio went to the statue and did so. Naibis then said, "Rama, go to the Madonna and pick up the December Book I've just put there." Rama went to the statue and did so. Naibis took a deep breath. "Now, exchange Words. Evoke!"

Agio went over to the statue of the Pieta and gently placed the

December Book on her lap. Rama, in turn, placed the March Book on the Madonna's lap.

The Circle of Readers reacted violently. "No! No! Stop!" they shouted. Some were so angry that they stood up and pointed at Naibis and yelled, "Desecrator." Several Readers were looking at the door as if they were about to walk out. "Oh no, not again." I thought.

Then Naibis put her finger to her lips and said, "Please, friends. Please be quiet. Look at the Two Readers. Look at what is happening.

People thought Naibis was talking about Agio and Rama. They looked at the two men. "No," Naibis said. "Look there at those Two Readers," and she pointed to the Madonna and the Pieta. All of the Readers turned their heads toward the statues. The entire roomful of people knelt down.

The red book was giving a strange wonderful luster to the green Madonna.

The green book was giving a strange wonderful luster to the red Pieta.

"*Capax Dei*," said Naibis. And she went over to the statues and stood between them right in the middle of the lustrous brightness and said, "*Capax Lumen*."

Standing in the halo she had created Naibis said, "Will you now let me finish the How-Can-This-Be Homily?" The Readers nodded and got up off the ground and sat in their seats.

> And so in time, young Rama was able to make his the words of R. G. Marie who responded to her own question, "How can this be?" with, "Be this (redness) done to me!"

> And so in time young Agio was able to make his the words of R. G. Marie who responded to her own question, "How can this be?" with, "Be this (greenness)

done to me!"

We saw all this unfold when the two young men discovered their respective vocations.

But let's stay with the question a little longer. In midlife the reference for *this* changes in Rama's view of things; at midlife the Redbead asks, "How can this be?" in reference to the world of joy.

Likewise, in midlife the reference for *this* changes in Agio's view of things; at midlife the Greenbead asks, "How can this be?" in reference to the world of sorrow.

And then what happens?

The one who knows the response to "How can this much joy be?" is sent by R. G. Marie to the middle-aged Rama.

The one who knows the response to "How can this much sorrow be?" is sent by R. G. Marie to the middle-aged Agio.

Now you can see how Lady Enantiodromia works.

The wedding of opposites is a great event in the history of the Circle of Readers. We need each other because we cannot fully answer the question, "How can this be?" with a reply from Red

Marie alone. Likewise we cannot fully
answer the question, "How can this be?"
with a reply from Green Marie alone.

We need both eyes of the whole Red/
Green Marie if we are to lectio this world
of joys and sorrows; yes, we need R. G.
R.G.[12] Marie if we want to be big-
souled, *Mahatma*, if we want to be whole
and complete.

Naibis then handed out two poems which she had written for
the occasion and asked the reunited Readers to take five minutes
and quietly lectio them.

THE FIFTEENTH READING
Beware of Fundamentalism

By Naibis

A page of simplistic word
is depthless, bodiless,
non-incarnate.

A page of complex word
is dense, bodiful,
incarnate.

***Choose the incarnate, welcome
complexity!***

The incarnate Word is light and dark;

---

[12] *R.G. R.G. Marie* - Red-Green Readers-Guide Marie.

the incarnate Word is ordered and wild.

Once incarnate, contextual, the Word
becomes paradoxical.

Look at what it did to R. G. Marie.
When the Word imprinted her
she became Virgin and Mother.

A page of complex word
asks the reader to participate;
to say, "Yes."

The reader then becomes,
as she was,
a glorious book that...

Opens and Encloses
the paradoxical
beauty-full truth.

Whatever is contextually true
must by necessity be
paradoxical.

If you want to be contextually true,
the Word in this world,
you must by necessity be ...

Green and Red,
Virgin and Mother:
A Glorious Book which ...

Opens and Encloses
the paradoxical
beauty-full truth.

R.G. Marie

When she gave the Word a body
    and made it weighty,
R.G. gave us simultaneously
    a mine to make us wealthy;
But the glorious gold is found only
    by Reading the odd-couple rosary.

THE SIXTEENTH READING
Mary of Nazareth Made the Word Readable

By Naibis

You, too, are to make the Word readable,
Are to contextualize it in your life,
Are to express it in your own way,
Are to give it a form and a body
It has never had.

An enormous innovation
Is expected of you.
Fabulous and dangerous
The freedom you have.

And see
How daring the Word is,
Risking itself in you.

It risks being misread.
But such its' love for new forms
That it takes the risk.

Just look 'round at these people,
My God! What variety,
What mad risk.

An enormous innovation
is expected of you.
Be a new and daring poem
Worthy of the risk-taking Word.

Naibis then nodded at me and I said to the Circle of Readers, "We will now continue the Jubilee Rosary. We have reached the Glorious Mysteries. Please turn to the person you are sitting next to and listen to five Great Hopes they have for the New Millennium.

"One personal hope, what's the most glorious that could happen;

"Two national hopes, what are the most glorious that could happen in Kenya;

"Two global hopes, what are the most glorious that could happen worldwide."

Naibis went from group to group listening to their great hopes. Then she stood in the middle of the room and said, "I have heard various great hopes as I walked around the room but the one great hope I heard most often is that activists and artists would imagine the future together and build it together. This will require courage, innovation always does. Be brave as first Eve and second Eve. For a thousand years first Eve chose a standing-up mate. She was bold and innovative, for indeed she was making a funny choice.

"The first Eve and her daughters chose males who related well and cooperated well. They chose mates who stood on two legs and could use their arms *for carrying the children*.

"One and a half million years ago right here in the Rift Valley the first millennia of Eves said 'Yes' to the most Christlike, clownish males and this made the face of humanity shine ever brighter. But it took courage because The Stalwarts of Ape Society must have disapproved of their choice. It was so irregular, abnormal, and unnatural.

"Then Second Eve said 'Yes' to the fullest humanity imaginable in choosing the Holy fool, the ultimate human being, Jesus Christ. We her followers must also choose the humane, we must select what is most Christlike. That is how we move human evolution forward. We just have to keep choosing the foolish and more complete human being; someone like Lwanga, a Jester-sage.

"The Social Forms we say 'Yes' to, in the new century, might also be scarey. But these cultural 'mutations'/holy innovations will move our species forward. Stand fast when the Stalwarts of Society tell you these new social forms are dangerous; irregular, abnormal, etc. Be brave!

"The Circle of Readers is a good example of a **dangerous, innovative social form**. Never before have rosarian artists and activists come *together* this way; reading beads together, and laughing."

"The crowning point of human evolution is laughter. No other creature has evolved to this point—to laugh at itself. One observes how serious all the other animals are, so serious and sad.

"The 1st Eves had a sufficient sense of humor that they could see something beautiful in the absurd standing males, and that sense of humor, little as it was, got human evolution started. We activists and contemplatives sharing full hearted, tear filled laughter, we are the fulfillment of the human project – we crown it. Laughter is the fruit of Consciousness; and its fullest expression."

Then Naibis sat down and I jumped to my feet, my blessed two feet, and said, "We are now going to pray the Glorious Decade. Keep you Great Hopes in mind, and let us pray together this 'Hail Mary.'"

> Hail Rainbow Mary,
> Full of Glory,
> The Lord is with you.
>
> Blessed are you among innovators
> And blessed your greatest dream
> - The Biggest Hope of All-
> Jesus the Word.
>
> Lady of Irony,
> Sage of Reversal
> Pray for us Readers
> Now and at the Hour
> We see Irony in the glass
> Our opposite, and laugh.

When the Glorious Decade was over and the room became

quiet again, I looked around the circle of Readers and said, "We have finished our reading of the Jubilee Rosary, and we have finished our celebration of the Wedding of Opposites."

I turned toward the ruby-emerald luster in which Rama and Agio sat. "Is there anything more you two Readers want to say before we leave today?"

Rama and Agio nodded. They stood up, and faced each other. Rama was wearing his doctor robes and holding an immunization needle. Agio was wearing his painter robes and holding a paint brush.

For a full minute they gazed lovingly at one another. Then they bowed to each other, and said, "*Mahatma*."

I thought everything that could be said had been said but the Two Readers surprised me. They turned to me, and proclaimed, "If we are *Mahatma* it is because of Taak."

I wasn't sure if they were speaking of Taak, my baby brother or if they were speaking of Taak, the blessing, or both.

But of this I am sure: the best word I could put at the end of this millennial edition of the Wasomaji, the only word that makes it complete, is *Taak*.

Envoi

by Liberita and Naibis

Throughout this book we have given illustrations of Enantiodromia: the yearning in a thing for holiness; the desire in a thing to become or evoke its opposite. By now we hope you realize that there is a built-in *bacchanalia* to everything. Nature loves a *Mardi gras*.

But, still, the character of a thing abides. Red is basically red, and Green is basically green.

Red, though, is not the old color it was. See, it is a stranger, richer, more lustrous Red; we might even say it's verdant Red.

And, Green, too, is not the old color it was. See, it is a stranger, richer, more lustrous Green; we might even say it is ruddy Green.

In reading our compilation of the writings of Rama and Agio we hope that you (whether you be a Redbead or a Greenbead) have had a little vacation from your self, have had your own *bacchanalia*. And though you are basically who you were before reading this book, we do hope that our anthology has made you feel a little more complete – stranger, richer, and more lustrous.

If not, may you soon have the good fortune of the monk who said that the best day of his life was the day a lucky wind blew off his halo (shattering his hagiography into pieces like an egg).

May the force of Enantiodromia, a force that cannot be contained, hatch you and hatch you and hatch you until there's nothing left of your caricature to crack and you can proudly say as God says: "I am who I am."

We challenge you with the first word of the blessing that the Maasai use when they lift up a newborn child into the sun's undivided and glorious light, **Taak...: Be Your Full Self!**

Peter Daino, S.M., is a Marianist Brother who has worked extensively in Africa. A native of Endwell, NY, he first went to Africa during the mid seventies with the Peace Corps. While there, in Niger, he met the Marianists who were planting trees to stop the desertification of the Sahel. Peter returned to the United States and earned a Master's Degree in Education from the University of Dayton. While there he entered the Society of Mary, became a Brother and was missioned to Africa. Peter worked in Nairobi, Kenya, for 17 years, and helped to start several community development projects in the slums of that city. Peter also holds a Master's Degree in Marian Theology from the International Marian Research Institute of the University of Dayton. He has recently begun a new work in Malawi, teaching literacy and building a vocational training center for orphans. The center was named by Peter's mother 8,000 miles away in New York in the final weeks of her struggle with cancer. She called it the Miracle because to every prayer, and to every sacrifice there is an answer, she said, though often it is not the one expected.

Brother Daino has published two other books, *Stabat Mater,* and *Mary: Mother of Sorrows, Mother of Defiance.*